the GENTILE

VALLEY *of* BONES

the GENTILE
VALLEY *of* BONES

JOHN G. ROGERS

TATE PUBLISHING & Enterprises

Published by Tate Publishing & Enterprises, LLC
127 E. Trade Center Terrace | Mustang, Oklahoma 73064 USA
1.888.361.9473 | www.tatepublishing.com

Tate Publishing is committed to excellence in the publishing industry. The company reflects the philosophy established by the founders, based on Psalm 68:11,
"The Lord gave the word and great was the company of those who published it."

Book design copyright © 2010 by Tate Publishing, LLC. All rights reserved.
Cover design by Kellie Southerland
Interior design by Jeff Fisher

Published in the United States of America

ISBN: 978-1-61663-164-2
Religion, Biblical Studies, History & Culture
10.04.06

Dedication

Many people have influenced my life and ministry, and I would like to acknowledge some of them who, by their help and assistance, have given me encouragement to study the Word of God, minister it to others, and put some of my teachings into written form.

The first and greatest influence on my personal and spiritual life came from my parents, James E. and Lucy J. Rogers, who have long since gone to glory. From their dedication of me to God at birth, throughout our family life, and into my educational training, they maintained a home in which Bible reading and prayer, morning and evening, was practiced daily. They sacrificially sent me from Kansas to Georgia to a Bible school when I was in high school and influenced me to attend Southwestern Bible College and Oklahoma City University.

I also dedicate this book to my wife, Margie, who has encouraged and prayerfully supported me in the teaching ministry. My brother, Thomas Aaron, my sister, Gloria Faith, and their spouses have always given me their prayerful support. Those who have faithfully attended our Bible study classes have inspired me with their faithful participation, generous financial support for activities and projects of my ministry, and the printing of this book. To all of them, I gratefully dedicate this book.

Among those who have provided personal assistance throughout the development of this book, my previous book, and the hundreds of lessons we have distributed over the past decade is Jack Curtiss, my computer guide and producer of scores of CDs, and Lola Tippin, who has dedicated many hours of her time to proofing materials I have given her. To both of them, I say, *thank you!*

TABLE OF CONTENTS

Introduction	9
In the Beginning	13
The Creative Works Beginning in Genesis 1:2	25
The Crown of the Creation	37
The Creation of Marriage	45
The Fall of Man	51
The Establishment of Families	79
The Development of Civilization	91
Tribes Were Developed	97
The Development of Cities and Nations	103
God's Declares His Disappointment with Man	109
God's Destructive Action Against Sin	119

God's Judgment against Man at Babel   127

Abraham is Separated
     from the Gentile Nations   133

The Gentile Nations from
     the Abrahamic Covenant to Christ   139

The Gentile Hope   149

The Gentile Valley of Bones   155

Final Judgments of God Against Man's Sins   167

INTRODUCTION

For more than fifty years, I have been teaching the Word of God. During these years, I have taught a series of lessons on prophecy as well as many other biblical subjects.

For the past nine years, I have been teaching a Monday night Bible class that began when my pastor asked me to devote those lessons to the Book of Revelation. It is from those lessons that I have come to know, enjoy, and appreciate a large number of people who have a deep interest in this study.

As a part of that series of lessons, I taught one lesson on the restoration of "Ezekiel's Valley of Dry Bones." That lesson was well received, and I was encouraged to put it into print as a booklet, simple and plain enough anyone could read it, understand it, and convey its message to others. It was completed in 2007, and has been distributed from Maine to Washington, from Florida to California.

This past year, as I was continuing the Monday night Bible class lessons, I decided to do a lesson on the Gentile Valley of Bones, as a sequel to the first book. When we were studying the lesson on Armageddon, it came to my mind that there were similarities, yet great differences, in these two pictures. Ezekiel's Valley of Dry Bones had developed over a long period of time, but the Gentile Valley of Bones developed under the judgment of the rider on the white horse at the end of Armageddon. Hence, the word *dry* is not involved, as these bodies had not been in this valley a long time. Throughout the tribulation, great destruction from God and from one another would come to the Gentiles, but only at Armageddon would there be a valley where the Gentiles' bones would represent their final end.

Ezekiel's Valley of Dry Bones Lives Again represents the gathering of Israel to the promised land from among the nations of the world. Their restoration in 1948 signaled their national and governmental rebirth, and the completion of their spiritual restoration will happen when they accept Jesus Christ as their Messiah after Armageddon. They will inhabit the earth during the millennial reign of Jesus Christ, and through him, inherit the renewed earth to inhabit forever and ever.

The Gentile Valley of Bones can claim no national restoration to life, because they become a feast for the fowls of the air God calls from around the world. In the second chapter of Daniel, they are pictured as being ground as "chaff of the summer threshing floors, and the wind carried them away that no place was found for them." Their resurrection will only come at the time of the "white throne judgment," where they will be condemned to eternal death and cast into the eternal suffering and torment of the lake of fire, meaning they will never get over dying. The righteous, who have inherited eternal life, will never get over living. It was this great contrast in their eternal destiny that inspired me to write this lesson and develop this book. I hope it will be a blessing.

In the Beginning

In the beginning God created the heaven and the earth.

Genesis 1:1

Thus the heavens and the earth were finished and all the host of them.

Genesis 2:1

And I saw an angel standing in the sun; and he cried with a loud voice, saying to all the fowls that fly in the midst of heaven, Come and gather yourselves together unto the supper of the great God. That ye may eat the flesh of kings, and the flesh of captains, and the flesh of mighty men, and the flesh of horses, and of them that sit on them, and the flesh of all men, both free and bond, both small and great. And the remnant were slain with the sword of him that sat upon the horse, which sword proceeded out of his mouth, and all the fowls were filled with their flesh.

Revelation 19:17–18 and 21

With these few words of these three chapters, God introduces His creative works, places them at the beginning of all things, and establishes His rights to them as their Creator. Then, with only a few more words, He discloses to John how they end.

"In the beginning" means only God the Creator existed prior to this. This heaven and earth existed prior to all other created things. All other created things described, referred to, or spoken of would follow this first act of creation. This is as simple, as absolute, and as descriptive as it could be made and is followed by, but not dependent upon, the further description of God's creative works, beginning in Genesis 1:2.

Genesis 1:1 presupposes the prior eternal existence of God, which is described in the Scriptures as a Trinity of God the Father, God the Son, and God the Holy Ghost. Only this eternal Trinity can claim being "from everlasting to everlasting," Psalms 90:2 says, "Before the mountains were brought forth, or ever thou hadst formed the earth and the world, even from everlasting to everlasting, thou art God." Also Habakkuk 1:12 says, "Art thou not from everlasting, O Lord my God, mine Holy One?"

Many of the things that describe and identify God are provided through Him or done by Him and will be everlasting, but the Triune God is the only person or thing that combines "without beginning and without end." Only the Triune God has inhabited eternity past, because He is omnipresent. That means He was before all things, He is now, and He will be in the eternal future. However, as the omniscient and omnipotent God, He has also surrounded Himself with His created works, beginning with the heaven and the earth and all that He has placed within them, and they will be a part of the eternal future.

Any look at the first heaven and earth must begin with a look at their Creator and founder. Unless we begin in truth, we will face many unanswerable questions, project many false theories, come to many wrong conclusions, and will be unable to prove whether they are truly unanswerable, blatantly false, or ignorantly erroneous.

When we believe in and accept what many call the creation theory, that God created the heaven and the earth and all that is within them, we can answer the unanswerable questions, we can disprove the false theories, and we can correct the false conclusions.

The Creator

Genesis 1:1 identifies God (Elohim) as Creator. *Elohim* is the word we use to describe one of the aspects of God. It means "one who is strong," "one who is mighty as a leader," "one who rules as the supreme deity."

When we identify God, or Elohim, as the Creator of heaven and earth, we deny atheism, for He exists separate from and above the spirit of man. When we identify God, or Elohim, as the Creator, we deny polytheism, for it was not gods who were the creators of the heaven and the earth, but God. When we identify God, or Elohim, as the Creator, we deny evolution, because the solar system is not the result of a big bang explosion of compressed, rotating protons and neutrons. The belief that God, or Elohim, created all things denies that life began entirely by happenstance, and at some time in the past, a single living cell appeared from non-living matter and from this one cell all other living forms of life appeared.

The Fact of Creation

The belief that God, or Elohim, created the heaven and the earth establishes the fact of creation and provides the most elemental descriptions of it. We accept as a fact what the writer says in Hebrews 11:3: "Through faith we understand that the worlds were framed by the Word of God, so that things which are seen were not made of things which do appear." John further explains this in John 1:3: "All things were made by Him, and without Him was not any thing made that was made."

We must have faith that there is a God; that He is from everlasting to everlasting, or *omnipresent;* that He is all powerful, or *omnipotent;* and that He has the wisdom, knowledge, and understanding, or *omniscience,* to create the earth and heavens, and all this is within them. By this faith, we believe He created what the heaven and the earth were made of; therefore, "they were not made of things which do appear" (Hebrews 11:3). Without this faith, man can never satisfactorily and ineradicably explain the heaven(s) and the earth and all that is within them.

If we believe that God alone is from everlasting to everlasting, and believe these three attributes belong to God alone, and that no other being existed prior to Genesis 1:1, then we are compelled to believe in and accept God's Word as to the creation of all things in both heaven and earth.

If what I have just stated is true, we must also accept as a fact that God's Word establishes the fact of creation but has reserved the when, or as we would like to say, time of creation, to Himself and possibly for future revelation when the limitations of this earthly being receives perfection as promised in I Corinthians 13:10. He may also have reserved within the strata of the earth, for future revelation, physical evidences of past inhabitants of the earth prior to the creative works beginning in Genesis 1:2. Should that happen, if He so chose, He could allow those perfected to understand the when, what, how, and why of that creation. Until, or if, that should happen, God wants us to be living Godly lives now and looking forward to the new heaven and new earth, not back to the old, which did not and does not pertain to His relationship with us.

What Do We Know About This First Creation?

When did that creation take place? We do not know when this specific work of creation took place. There was no man there as an observer or as a recorder to provide a record of it. It was before time; therefore, God has given no measurement for man to know a specific date, age, or era when it was created.

There could have been a long period between the Genesis 1:1 work of creation and the Genesis 1:2–31 works of creation, with their completion recorded in Genesis 2:1, "Thus the heavens and the earth were finished, and all the hosts of them." Notice I said a long period between these works, because time had not yet begun.

How long did it exist? We do not know how long it existed. It could have existed from its point of creation somewhere in the eternal past and could have continued until some point before its recreation, beginning in Genesis 1:2.

We do not know how long after God created the heaven of Genesis 1:1 until He created angels to inhabit it. Neither do we know how long after He created this earth that He began the process of creating and filling it with the creatures that would inhabit it.

We do not know how long those creatures existed, and neither do we know exactly how and when their end came. Many theories exist, and the preserved evidence seems to support some of these theories, but God Himself has not referred to them nor given direct confirmation on any of it.

What was that creation like? We have limited information and evidence of when and how that creation took place, as well as precisely what it was. From God's command to Adam and Eve, "Be fruitful, and multiply and replenish the earth" (Genesis 1:28), we are led to believe it was populated with living creatures.

Adam was to replace by *replenishing* the earth with what may have been a creature that had some level of intellect and leadership greater that any other creature, yet never reached Adam's level of development, wisdom, power, or authority, because they were not created in the image and after the likeness of God (Genesis 1:26). Since we are given none of their characteristics, nature, or appearance, and whether they had any spiritual qualities, we can only speculate on what that creature was like. Did Adam bear any likeness or resemblance to that which he was to replace? Had God wanted us to know, He would have revealed more to us.

The created *image* and *likeness* of God could refer specifically and only to the spiritual, moral, and intellectual *image* and *likeness* of God. "God is a Spirit; and they that worship him must worship him in spirit and in truth" (John 4:24). When man dies, the spirit returns to God who gave it, but the soul and body face eternal death, unless they have been redeemed, changed, and received eternal life. It was for this very purpose that "God so loved the world, that he gave his only begotten Son, that whosoever believeth in him should not perish, but have everlasting life" (John 3:16).

The physical body was created from the dust of the earth, making it a mortal body. Only when this mortal body is changed by spiritual quickening, resurrection, and is translated by the rapture will His likeness be completed in it. Romans 8:11 begins this process: "But if the Spirit of him that raised up Jesus from the dead dwell in you, he that raised up Christ from the dead shall also quicken your mortal bodies by his Spirit that dwelleth in you." For those to whom this quickening has come, I Corinthians 15:51–54 shows the final steps in this process:

> Behold, I shew you a mystery, We shall not all sleep, but we shall all be changed. In a moment, in the twinkling of an eye, at the last trump; for the trumpet shall sound, and the dead shall be raised incorruptible, and we shall be changed. For this corruptible must put on incorruption, and this mortal must put on immortality. So when this corruptible shall have put on incorruption, and this mortal shall have put on immortality, then shall be brought to pass the saying that is written, Death is swallowed up in victory.

When this happens, this mortal body shall have completed its change to a spiritual body, suitable for its place in heaven and its place with Christ on His throne. Philippians 3:20–21 tells us when this final and eternal change takes place: "For our conversation is in heaven; from whence also we look for the Savior, the Lord Jesus Christ. Who shall change our vile body, that it may be fashioned like unto his glorious body, according to the working whereby he is able even to subdue all things unto himself."

This could also help answer some of the questions and problems concerning the theory of man having *evolved* from an ape-like creature to what Adam was at the very first moment of his creation. The answer is simple, if we believe that God created what was on the earth prior to Genesis 1:2, and that He also created all that was upon the earth after Genesis 1:2; therefore, one did not evolve from the other. They were different, although there could have been some general likeness in structure, carriage, and stature, especially since God specifically directed Adam and Eve to *replenish,* which means to *replace* them. The difference was that God created Adam as a more perfect being when He created him in His own *image* and His own *likeness.* This accounts for the spiritual nature of Adam that none of the other creatures have.

The purpose for which God created and equipped Adam also accounts for the higher level and state of

Adam's physical being, knowledge, wisdom, understanding, and potential from those whose bones may bear some resemblance to Adam, but were not spiritually created in God's image and likeness; nor were they created for the purpose of being the *crown* of this creation. Therefore, never could they develop to Adam's beginning state of perfection and God-likeness, nor could they develop to the level to "subdue the earth" and have "dominion over the fish of the sea, and over the fowl of the air, and over every living thing that moveth upon the earth" (Genesis 1:28). These things are true, whether or not you believe God created all things, with man as the *crown* of this creation, instead of man having evolved from some other creature.

Within the strata of the earth, God has preserved evidence of that past creation. The ascending layers of this strata indicate it was a progressive work, but with creatures much different from those of the earth Adam was to "subdue and have dominion" over. These preserved specimens indicate that great varieties of organic as well as biological or creature beings had been created; however, not one has been found that shows evidence of the degree of intellectual nature, level of control over the earth and its other creatures, nor the level of perfection God placed in man, the *crown* of this new creation, beginning in Genesis 1:2.

What happened to them? We do not know what happened to them, other than indications that something catastrophic suddenly ended that creation, leaving the earth as it was found in Genesis 1:2: "And the earth was without form and void, and darkness was upon the face of the deep." Many believe there is only one record of anything that could have been so destructive, so confusing, so forceful as to destroy that creation, coming so suddenly that some of the creatures still had food in their mouths, coming so forcefully that the land and waters became intermingled, throwing everything into chaos.

Some believe that one thing was God casting Lucifer and the rebellious angels out of heaven. Luke 10:18 says, "And He said unto them, I beheld Satan as lightning fall from heaven." I Corinthians 14:33 says, "For God is not the author of confusion, but of peace, as in all churches of the saints." Satan must then be the *author of confusion*. If so, God cast him out of heaven to preserve the peace, holiness, harmony, and unity of His heavenly kingdom, as well as its place in His overall kingdom plan and purpose.

This total cleansing of Lucifer (Satan) and his followers from heaven, together with their powerful forces of evil and wickedness, could have enveloped the earth in total darkness, because when God's presence is withdrawn, total darkness is the result. Where Satan is present, confusion, destruction, and chaos reign. Except for the divine forces of God, which He could have sent in judgmental powers, no forces other than the powers of Satan could have brought such destruction. We do not know whether God will ever reveal this.

How long has it been since this happened? We do not know, for we do not know how long the period was between Genesis 1:1 and 1:2. As previously stated, it could have been a long period, or one closely following the other. Evidently God felt that was not, or should not be, of importance to us, but only what is stated in the two scriptures above and what followed them should be of our concern.

Parts of these paragraphs are taken from my lessons on the "Millennial Kingdom" and "The New Heaven and the New Earth." This provides the background and the basic premise upon which the remainder of this book is founded.

The Creative Works Beginning in Genesis 1:2

We have established that the heaven and the earth were created "in the beginning" (Genesis 1:1). We further know that at some point in the eternal past, on this first earth referred to, God began a process of creation, but something brought about a total destruction of all that had been created on it. Out of the chaos of that destruction, we see the beginning of His creative works referred to from Genesis 1:2 to Genesis 2:1.

The measurement God used to identify the progression of this new creative work He called *days*. This will be discussed in more detail a little later on.

For the first three days of this creative work, God Himself was the light. On the beginning of the fourth day, He created what would become the source of natural light on the earth. Within that process, He also established time and separated it into hours, more clearly defining days and nights. This creation was completed within six days, and on the seventh day, "God rested from all the works which He had made" (Genesis 2:2).

Within these six days of creation, God built the infrastructure that would accommodate and sustain the creature life He would create to conclude these creative works. He would then, as His last creative act, create the crowning work of these six days by creating man in His own likeness and in His own image and creating woman from the man.

Let us take a brief look at this process. Genesis 1:2 says, "And the earth was without form and void, and darkness was upon the face of the deep." This indicates that prior to the beginning of the creative works of these six days, chaos and confusion reigned. The earth already existed but was without form, indicating total lack of organization and purpose, having nothing that reflected the omnipresence of God.

It was also void, indicating it was empty, having nothing that reflected the omnipotence and omniscience of God. "Darkness was upon the face of the deep." This describes the opposite of that which resembled and reflected the presence of the essence of God, for "God is light, and in Him is no darkness" (I John 1:5). That same essence identified Jesus

Christ as a part of the Trinity, when He said, "I am the light of the world."

The earth and water were commingled into nothing but a deep, murky mass, surrounded by darkness, with nothing that glorified God or that He could be glorified in.

It was at this point God began to speak, and by the power, will, and wisdom of these words, the chaos, confusion, emptiness, and darkness ended. Within only six of what God would designate as *days,* the conditions, environment, ingredients, and essential processes that would reflect the glory, power, wisdom, and presence of His attributes would be manifested.

The first action of God, beginning with the works of the first day, was *geological.* There were three essentials for plant, vegetable, and creature life to be on the earth. In these first three days, these three would be separated, controlled, and utilized in this creative process.

First: "God said, Let there be light, and there was light." This light was directly from the essence of God Himself. It was not *astrological* light. He had not created, made, or formed any other source of light on the first day. It was not until the fourth day that God created and turned on the astrological lights of the heavens.

Three things that His light does would become essential for life on the earth. (1) Light *reveals.* His light would be the only light for the first three days. Without this light as the first act of these six days of creation, any other creative work would not be seen. All plant life needs light, and since these were created on the third day, He provided them light from the essence of Himself. This light also revealed God's knowledge, wisdom, power, and glory each day, as it revealed His creative works for that day. (2) Light *sustains* organic life. Without light, the creative work of the third day could not have survived. Genesis 1:11–12 provides a description of the creation of all organic things that would grow from the ground and that were created to sustain the creature life He would create in succeeding days. God knew He was going to create man from the earth and that man would need food to live, so He created organic life from the earth that would be compatible to the nutritional needs of man and to the creatures that would become a part of man's food chain. Light also sustains spiritual life. He who walks in darkness "knoweth not whether he goeth. While ye have light, believe in the light, that ye may be the children of light" (John 12:35–36). I Thessalonians 5:5 says, "Ye are all the children of light, and the children of the day. We are not of the night nor of the darkness." (3) Light *warms*. To sustain the creature life God was planning to create on the earth, warmth was another essential element. Within the past history of the world, there is identified what has been called the *ice age*. Could it be that at the time of the chaotic destruction of the previous creation, darkness became so complete that temperatures dropped so drastically, so suddenly, it was almost an instant deep freeze? A long time ago, I heard someone tell how cold the earth would become within forty-eight hours if suddenly light from the sun, moon, and stars ceased. It was almost incomprehensible.

Warmth is thought of in physical, mental, emotional, and spiritual terms. The light that God created provides one or more of these to each of the creatures He has placed on the earth. In every case, it is pleasant, peaceful, and necessary.

Second: On the second day, God said, "Let there be a firmament in the midst of the waters, and let it divide the waters from the waters. And God made the firmament, and divided the waters which were under the firmament from the waters which were above the firmament; and it was so" (Genesis 1:6–7).

This was the creation of what we call the *atmospheric.* Verse eight: "And God called the firmament Heaven. And the evening and the morning were the second day." Within this firmament, God used air to separate the waters of the earth from the waters of this heaven.

It would also be the place Satan would be identified with as the "prince of the power of the air" (Ephesians 2:2). We do not know when this title came to him, but we can believe that with each of God's creative acts, Satan wasted no time in attempting to exert power and authority within this atmospheric heaven, and, by this name, sought to wrest control of it from God. Man had not yet been created, so Satan had not yet learned whether God was creating it for Himself or another. Neither did he yet know what else God would create.

As God progressively built the infrastructure of the kingdom, He was building upon the earth; this firmament of the second day would do several things.

It would provide the clouds where rain would be formed, stored, and then released to help sustain life upon the earth. The waters that were within the bounds of the seas and rivers could not reach the dry land to sustain life. God used waters that were under the earth as a mist or dew for plant life, but this would not suffice to sustain creature life as they roamed the earth. It would be from this firmament that rain would be released to cover the earth, providing its essential elements to this new creation.

God would, at some future time, use the waters of the firmament for judgment, as well as blessings. From this firmament, or atmospheric heaven, lightning, thunder, hail, and violent storms over both water and land would come. It would be the source of divine judgment upon the earth for the wickedness of man in Noah's day. It will be included as a source of divine judgment during the last days and during the tribulation. Lightning symbolizes the destructive element that God uses as judgment against all who become Satan's followers at the close of the millennial reign.

Revelation 20:7–9 says:

> And when the thousand years are expired, Satan shall be loosed out of his prison. And shall go out to deceive the nations which are in the four quarters of the earth, Gog and Magog, to gather them together to battle; the number of whom is as the sand of the sea. And they went up on the breadth of the earth, and compassed the camp of the saints about, and the beloved city; and fire came down from God out of heaven, and devoured them.

It was in the atmospheric heaven that God established the bow as the token of His everlasting covenant with Noah that He would not destroy the earth by water again (Genesis 9:11–17).

It will be through the planetary heaven and this firmament heaven that the dead in Christ, together with the living saints, shall be caught up to be with the Lord in the place He has gone to prepare for them in the heaven of heavens.

I Thessalonians 4:16–17 says:

> For the Lord himself shall descend from heaven with a shout, with the voice of the archangel, and with the trump of God: and the dead in Christ shall rise first. Then we which are alive and remain shall be caught up together with them in the clouds, to meet the Lord in the air; and so shall we ever be with the Lord.

What an important part this firmament has had and will have in the eternal picture of the earth and man.

Third: On the third day, God developed the basics of the *geographical* map of the earth.

Genesis 1:9–10 says:

> And God said, Let the waters under the heaven be gathered together unto one place, and let the dry land appear: and it was so. And God called the dry land Earth; and the gathering together of the waters called he Seas, and God saw that it was good.

When dry land appeared and the water became the seas, God established the boundaries for both, thus creating the original geographical map of the earth. Remember, prior to this, "the earth was without form and void, and darkness was upon the face of the deep" (Genesis 1:2). The term *dry land* clearly indicates the separation of water from the land; step by step, God was preparing this planet for the display of His wisdom, power, glory, and honor in His future creative works.

Dry land was another of the essentials to sustain the vegetable and creature life God had planned for the earth. On this third day, by His word, vegetable life begins the first stage of biological life.

Genesis 1:11–12 says:

> And God said, Let the earth bring forth grass, the herb yielding seed, and the fruit tree yield-ing fruit after his kind, whose seed is in itself

upon the earth: and it was so. And the earth brought forth grass, and herb yielding seed after his kind, and the tree yielding fruit, whose seed was in itself, after his kind: and God saw that it was good.

God would then use these three geological creations He had just completed—sea, air, and land—as the habitation for His next creation, the creature life. Genesis 1:20–25 presents the creation of sea, air, and land creatures. Each of the three geological creations had their organic, chemical, and geographical purposes to fulfill, and God had planned each of these purposes to be essential parts of the life He would place on it as living creatures.

What a marvelous picture of creation is unfolding. Notice the consistency of the creative works and how they prepare for, complement, and help sustain the next orders of creation, especially those to whom God would give creature life.

Fourth: On the fourth day, He would create the astrological system, or planetary heaven, consisting of the sun, moon, stars, and planets. The sun and moon were to divide the day from the night and would be for signs, seasons, and years (Genesis 1:14–16). Through their movement, much of the power to govern activities, growth, and life would be established.

This set in motion a system of day and night that was not dependent upon the repetition of the words, "And God said," but would systematically continue in their order upon this earth forever and ever. God confirmed this to Noah.

Genesis 8:22 says, "While the earth remaineth, seed time and harvest, cold and heat, summer and winter, and day and night shall not cease." Look at each of these individually. Seedtime and harvest represents *signs*. For centuries, people have looked at the signs before planting crops, and this would in turn control when they harvested those crops. Summer and winter represent seasons, as there are four seasons, with summer and winter being the apex of heat and cold, and fall and spring the ending of one and the beginning of the other. The days would be divided into what we now call weeks and months, with those culminating in years.

So much more could be said about this fourth day, but we simply look at it as God setting the earthly time clock that would ultimately merge with eternity. What He was creating would never cease to exist.

Fifth and sixth: On the fifth and sixth day, God created *genetic* and *biological* life. This would consist of inhabitants for air, sea, and land being created simply by God's Word. They were also the first of all the creation of these six days to have physical creature life. The vegetable creation had organic life, but that was not of the same nature as those with creature life (Genesis 1:20–25).

Within these verses, we see God complete the creation of all that He had planned to place within man's power, subordination, and control. With this creature life, man would not be alone on the earth, just as God Himself created angels in heaven who served, worshiped, obeyed, and honored Him. God knew it was not good to be alone.

In God's foreknowledge, He knew how the future multiple purposes of these creatures would serve man. They would not only serve man as companions and creatures to control but would become essential elements in man's daily life. For instance, God would use an animal to provide man his first acceptable clothing or covering. Genesis 3:21 says, "Unto Adam also and to his wife did the Lord God make coats of skins, and clothed them."

Adam and Eve had sewed fig leaves together to cover their nakedness, attesting to the fact their conscience had been awakened to evil (Genesis 3:7). God did not accept Adam using organic material as a covering to hide his sin and still his conscience, because it represented the works of man and did not involve creature sacrifice. God would only accept a blood sacrifice to restore life, for the life is in the blood. God Himself provided the first creature sacrifice when He provided the animal skins for Adam and Eve's covering. This was a symbol of the blood sacrifice His Son would make for man.

From that act of God, through Abel's sacrificial offering, God would honor the blood sacrifice. Genesis 4:4 says, "And Abel, he also brought of the firstlings of his flock and of the fat thereof. And the Lord had respect unto Abel and to his offering." This would continue through the animal sacrifices of the Old Testament until Jesus Christ came as the "Lamb of God, slain from the foundation of the world." Until He came, creature blood sacrifices were acceptable for the covering of man's sins.

The sacrificial blood of Jesus Christ brought in the new covenant. His blood sacrifice would eternally remove sin from those to whom it was applied. Hebrews 8:6 says, "By how much also he is the mediator of a better covenant;" verse 8 says, "Behold the days come, saith the Lord, when I will make a new covenant with the house of Israel and with the house of Judah." This would also provide the new testament, in Matthew 26:28: "For this is my blood of the new testament, which is shed for many for the remission of sins." See Mark 14:24 and Luke 22:20.

Some creatures would be used for thank offerings. Genesis 8:20 says, "And Noah builded an altar unto the Lord; and took of every clean beast, and of every clean fowl, and offered burnt offerings on the altar." They would also provide work and service. They would be ridden, provide milk, help tread out the corn, and perform many other services. Ultimately, they could all be used for food. First Timothy 4:4 says, "For every creature of God is good, and nothing to be refused, if it be received with thanks."

The Crown of the Creation

After creating the geological, geographical, astrological, agricultural, and biological infrastructure of the earthly creation, God then created the *genealogical* crown—man, with what we might call the *mini-attributes* of Godlikeness.

As the omnipresent God, He is "without beginning and without end." He is "from everlasting to everlasting." He inhabits eternity, with yesterday as today, and today as tomorrow, and tomorrow as yesterday. From the day God created the first man, Adam, man would not cease to exist. He would experience changes, limitations, and weaknesses, and because of his sin, would come under the penalty of death; however, this would not be an annihilation, but a judgmental punishment of eternal duration. The wages of sin is death. If man could get over dying without Jesus Christ, he could pay the wages for sin and become eligible for eternal life. Eternal life can only be received by accepting the eternal atonement Jesus Christ paid for our sins upon the cross.

As the omniscient God, He shared a degree of this omniscience with man more than with any of the other creatures. The entire plan, purpose, and ingredients of creation reflect this omniscience. One specific part of the omniscience of God that was placed on this earth, but that God restricted from man, was the tree of the knowledge of good and evil. God told Adam that in the day he ate thereof he would surely die (Genesis 2:16–17). God created man with a pure, innocent mind and a conscience that was only aware of that which was good. Had man obeyed this one restriction God had placed on him, he would never have known evil, his conscience would never have been awakened to guilt, and with no guilt, God's justice would never have brought judgment to man.

When Eve gave Adam fruit from that tree and he ate, Adam and all of his future generations, including Eve, came under the justice and judgment of God, requiring the penalty of death (Genesis 3:6). The body would die. "And Adam lived 930 years and he died" (Genesis 5:5). The soul would also die. "The soul that sinneth, it shall die" (Ezekiel 18:20). The spirit will return to God who gave it, but the body and soul will be punished with eternal death, in eternal torment in the lake of fire unless the person repents and accepts the death and blood of Jesus Christ as the atonement for his sins.

Adam began at the highest level of all creatures on earth. He was in the image and likeness of the King of kings and the Lord of lords (Genesis 1:27). He was given "dominion over the fish of the sea, and over the fowl of the air, and over the cattle, and over all the earth, and over every creeping thing that creepeth upon the earth" (Genesis 1:26). This required the highest degree of mental and physical powers of all creatures to rule over all the earth.

He was "made a little lower than the angels and crowned with glory and honor" (Psalms 8:5, Hebrews 2:7). Verse eight of Hebrews 2 says, "Thou hast put all things in subjection under his feet. For in that he put all in subjection under him, he left nothing that is not put under him."

Man was made up of body, soul, and spirit. This translates into physical, moral, and spiritual. The thing that blends the body and spirit and serves as the medium through which they can each express themselves is the soul. The body was created. The spirit was breathed into the body, at which time they became a living soul (Genesis 2:11). Though they were blended together, they retained their separate identities and functions. John 3:6 says, "That which is born of the flesh is flesh, and that which is born of the Spirit is spirit." The *living soul* becomes the channel through which the body and spirit are reflected, exercised, and accountable. When physical death comes, the blended body, soul, and spirit will be separated. The body shall return to the dust of the earth (Job 34:15), the spirit shall return to God who gave it (Ecclesiastes 12:7), and the soul will go to either paradise (Luke 23:43), or hell (Isaiah 5:14, 14:9; Luke 12:5), determined by whether they were still in their sins when death came or whether they had been born again through the atoning blood of Jesus Christ.

All of this combined—and there is much more—proves man was the result of, but not the limit of, divine planning, knowledge, purpose, and powers. Some may look upon this beginning as extremely elemental, of the most primitive nature, and only basic as it relates to the overall capabilities and possibilities human history has left evidence of having progressed through. This is true. God created man with all of the essential elements and authority to fulfill the commission He would give man, but it was up to man, operating within his own free-will, to obey God and fulfill this commission.

This is evolutionary only in the sense that God created man in His own likeness and His own image. This gave to man all of the inherent qualities, capabilities, possibilities, and ingredients he needed to develop himself, his environment, his possessions, and his powers to control the earth, its possessions, and its creatures into a highly complex, sophisticated, independent, morally and spiritually developed kingdom.

This initial creation provided man the mental powers, intellectual capacities, physical superiority, and self-confidence to command control over and submission from all creatures of the earth.

With the authority, approval, assistance, direction, spirit, and nature of the Creator, and in spite of the continuing interference of Satan from Eden to the millennium, man will advance until he shall have brought all things under his control. He will not do it through himself, through his own powers, through his own wisdom, or through his own righteousness. It will be twofold.

First, those who are overcomers and are raptured will be glorified, and by this, qualify to become the bride of Christ. As His bride, they have been promised to sit with Him upon His throne. Revelation 3:21 says, "To him that overcometh will I grant to sit with me in my throne, even as I also overcame, and am set down with my Father in his throne." They shall rule and reign with Him as kings and priests forever. Revelation 22:5 says, "And they shall reign for ever and ever."

Secondly, after the final cleansing of the earth by fire (Revelation 20:9), after Satan has been cast into the lake of fire (verse 10), after death and hell have been cast into the lake of fire (verse 14), after the final judgment has been passed (verse 15), and after the curse has been removed from the earth (Revelation 22:3), the redeemed mortals who entered the millennium, along with those who were born during the millennium and became saints, shall be immortal mortals and inherit the earth to eternally inhabit, possess, and replenish it.

Together with Jesus Christ, they will be the ones who shall fulfill the statement of Isaiah 9:6–7:

> For unto us a child is born, unto us a son is given; and the government shall be upon his shoulder; and his name shall be called Wonderful, Counselor, The mighty God, The everlasting Father, The Prince of Peace. Of the increase of his government and peace there shall be no end, upon the throne of David, and upon his kingdom, to order it, and to establish it with judgment and with justice from henceforth even for ever. The zeal of the Lord of hosts will perform this.

This progressive work in man can be traced through historical records and remains. If man leaves out a belief and faith in the God of the Genesis record of creation, he may come to the conclusion that it all happened through evolution alone. But when you add a belief in the existence and involvement of a God who is omnipresent (existing in the eternal past, in the present, and in the eternal future), a God who is omniscient (having all knowledge, all wisdom, all understanding, knowing all things past, present, and future), and a God who is omnipotent (having all power over everything in heaven, on earth, and under the earth, from everlasting to everlasting), you can see the image and likeness of God becoming clearer as man develops the potential God invested in him.

The progressive works of man have come by development of the innate, inherent wisdom, knowledge, and understanding he received from the One who created him. In spite of any credit man may take for this development, he is only developing the potentials with which his Creator endowed him and taking his rightful position and exercising the authority given him over all things God had created for him in the first six days of creation.

These things clearly establish the basic elements for the cycle of life God had intended for this crowning work of creation. With these, all other aspects of man that God created him for and endowed him with could develop. These would include his overall welfare, his culture, his relationships, and his spiritual life, as well as his power to rule the other creatures and worship his Creator.

Man's biological, physiological, psychological, and spiritual development, and his temporal welfare, were blessed by God. When God's commands are observed, His will performed and His plans carried out, His approval, blessing, and increase will happen. God's will for man in every one of these aspects is two fold: (1) "We all with open face, beholding as in a glass the glory of the Lord, are changed into the same image from glory to glory, even as by the Spirit of the Lord" (II Corinthians 3:18). (2) "That thou mayest prosper and be in health even as thy soul prospereth" (3 John 2). The first is development of that which God created in His own image, and the second is God's reward for spiritual service.

The Creation of Marriage

Adam became the genetic beginning of man on the earth. Soon God declared it was not good that man should be alone. Genesis 2:18 says, "And the Lord God said, It is not good that the man should be alone; I will make him an help meet for him."

Verses 21–25 say:

> And the Lord God caused a deep sleep to fall upon Adam, and he slept: and he took one of his ribs, and closed up the flesh instead thereof. And the rib, which the Lord God had taken from man, made he a woman, and brought her unto the man. And Adam said, This is now bone of my bones, and flesh of my flesh: she shall be called Woman, because she was taken out of man. Therefore shall a man leave his father and his mother, and shall cleave unto his wife; and they shall be one flesh. And they were both naked, the man and his wife, and were not ashamed.

Thus God created Eve, and these verses reveal the state of physical unity, moral purity, and spiritual innocence that bonded these two together.

God created Adam in His image and after His likeness. Eve was created from the rib of Adam, and this established his likeness in her. She was flesh of his flesh and bone of his bone. This gave her the physical elements of Adam, as well as God's breath and a living soul. What Adam was by creation, she became by creation, but God gave her a different position, purpose, responsibilities, accountability, and duties.

God wanted Adam to understand why He created Eve, what her relationship to him was, and what he was to be to her. As Adam's helpmeet, her purpose was different from that of Adam. Eve was an equal in service, an equal in relationship, and an equal in authority. In service, she was to bear children, helping fulfill the command to be "fruitful and multiply and replenish the earth." In relationship, they were to be "one flesh" (Genesis 2:24). Ruling with him, she would be his helpmeet. This pattern is carried through into the New Testament and is patterned after what God established as the relationship between Christ and the Church (Ephesians 5:21–33).

It was not until God punished Eve for sin that God told her, "I will greatly multiply thy sorrow and thy conception; in sorrow thou shalt bring forth children," and "thy desire shall be to thy husband, and he shall rule over thee" (Genesis 3:16).

Though God did not call this union a *marriage,* these verses clearly establish the basic standards for marriage. This union came about by the creative works of God and not by a formal action of man. In Genesis 2:24, Adam prophetically acknowledged the pledge of marriage and the first basic requirement of it, "Therefore shall a man leave his father and his mother, and shall cleave unto his wife; and they shall be one flesh."

This is the first time the word *wife* is used. Genesis 3:20 affirms the relationship of Adam and Eve as a marriage: "And Adam called his wife's name Eve; because she was the mother of all living." Here he called her his wife. The word *marriage* isn't used until Genesis 19:14, and there it is in the past tense, meaning it was already an established fact.

In the beginning, God created the creatures of the earth as both male and female for the purpose of propagating their species. This same pattern is followed with man, but because of man's superior position, his divine endowments, and personal responsibility and accountability to God for maintaining spiritual, physical, and moral purity, God established a higher relationship between Himself and man and between man and woman than He did between Himself and all other male and female creatures.

God has never forsaken this position with man. He declares He is married to Israel. Jeremiah 3:14 says, "Turn, O backsliding children, saith the Lord; for I am married unto you; and I will take you one of a city, and two of a family, and I will bring you to Zion." The redeemed of the earth are acknowledged as the wife of Jesus Christ, the Lamb. "Let us be glad and rejoice, and give honour to him, for the marriage of the Lamb is come, and his wife hath made herself ready" (Revelation 19:7).

God directed Noah to bring both male and female into the ark. Genesis 6:19–20 says, "And of every living thing of all flesh, two of every sort shalt thou bring into the ark, to keep them alive with thee; they shall be male and female. Of fowls after their kind, and of cattle after their kind, of every creeping thing of the earth after his kind, two of every sort shall come unto thee, to keep them alive." Verse 21 directed him to bring "all food that is eaten, and thou shalt gather it to thee; and it shall be for food for thee, and for them." When the flood abated, God renewed the command to "Be fruitful and multiply and replenish the earth" (Genesis 9:1, 7).

When God created angels, He did not create them as male and female, for He had no intention or plans for them to marry, to propagate, or to replenish heaven after Lucifer would deceive a third of them into following him in his rebellion against God and after God cast them out of heaven. They were a part of the family of God by creation, but they would not establish individual families of their own as man would on earth.

Angels were created as spiritual beings, just as God is Spirit. John 4:24 says, "God is a Spirit, and they that worship him must worship him in spirit and in truth." They were not created to rule over the physical earth but to serve, worship, and obey God in the heavenly, spiritual world. The only times when they have appeared to have physical bodies were when God sent them on specific assignments to the earth. In order for man to see them and communicate with them, they appeared in human form, but they were not human, for they were not born of human flesh as Jesus was.

God sent His Son, Christ, into this world to be the Savior of man; to fulfill this assignment, He had to take upon Himself human flesh. He became Jesus, the son of Mary, and by that, became the Son of man as well as being Christ, the Son of God. Had He not become this unity and taken a body of flesh and blood, He could never have fulfilled the requirement, "Without the shedding of blood is no remission" (Hebrews 9:22). After His resurrection, when He appeared to some of the disciples, they were so startled they thought they were seeing a spirit, but Jesus quickly dispelled that thought. Luke 24:39: "Behold my hands and my feet, that it is I myself: handle me, and see; for a spirit hath not flesh and bones, as ye see me have." He was identifying Himself to them as the same Jesus whom they had seen. He invited Thomas to touch Him, the physical Jesus, the son of Mary.

All this time He was also Christ, the Son of God. Jesus, the son of Mary, was the body through which Christ, the Son of God, could become the sacrifice for sin, taking the sting out of death and the victory out of the grave, but Christ, the Son of God, was the spirit through which Jesus, the son of Mary, could inherit and rule over the kingdom of God on earth. "Now this I say, brethren, flesh and blood cannot inherit the kingdom of God; neither doth corruption inherit incorruption" (1 Corinthians 15:50). In verses 51–57, Paul describes the change that shall take place "in a moment, in the winkling of an eye, at the last trump." That glorious event and those glorious changes are our eternal victory over the flesh, and verse 57 declares it comes "through our Lord Jesus Christ." These things will bring His bride to her marriage with the Lamb, where she becomes His wife and shall sit with Him in His throne to rule and reign with Him forever and ever.

THE FALL OF MAN

And God said, Let us make man in our image, after our likeness; and let them have domin-ion over the fish of the sea, and over the fowl of the air, and over the cattle, and over all the earth, and over every creeping thing that creep-eth upon the earth. So God created man in his own image, in the image of God created he him, male and female created he them.

Genesis 1:26–27

God reserved great honor, power, and position for this last act of the six days of creation. The honor was (verse 26) "Let us make man in our image, after our likeness.". The power was (verses 26 and 28) "Let them have dominion over" all of the previous created things, including the earth and "subdue it," includ-ing every creature. The position was as possessor of everything (verse 29) "Behold, I have given you," and then God clearly defines what all was encompassed within this gift.

Genesis 2 shows that God created Eve on the same day He created Adam. This also shows how quickly God responded to man's need for companionship and for a helpmeet. Genesis 2:18 says, "And the Lord God said, It is not good that the man should be alone; I will make him an helpmeet for him." Verses 21–22 records how God created this "helpmeet" and brought her to Adam.

Adam quickly recognized what God had done and who this was. Verse 23 says, "And Adam said, this is now bone of my bones, and flesh of my flesh: she shall be called Woman, because she was taken out of Man." He also immediately recognized what their relationship should be. Verse 24 says, "Therefore shall a man leave his father and his mother, and shall cleave unto his wife; and they shall be one flesh." Adam had no thought that anything would ever interfere with this relationship of instant love and devotion to one another. This was clearly the first case of love at first sight.

That which God had joined together through these two creative acts indicated no cause that would intimate this relationship could ever be broken, and this is what God intended. They were created in purity, innocence, and devotion to one another. Verse 25 says, "And they were both naked, the man and his wife, and were not ashamed." This state of purity and innocence meant they were created without any knowledge between good and evil. It was not until they sinned that they had the discernment between good and evil.

> And the Lord God called unto Adam, and said unto him, Where art thou? And he said, I heard thy voice in the garden, and I was afraid, because I was naked; and I hid myself. And he said, Who told thee thou wast naked? Hast thou eaten of the tree, whereof I commanded thee that thou shouldest not eat?
>
> Genesis 3:9–11

Beginning in this state of purity and innocence, they had no suspicion the inner parts of the earth held any evidence there could have been life on earth previously, what kind of life it could have been, and of what may have caused its disappearance. In their state of innocence, God had protected them from any concern of the past. The only hint of the past may have been in his command to them to be "fruitful and multiply, and replenish the earth" (Genesis 1:28).

They were also unaware that within the darkness of the world below them were the multitudes of fallen angels who had rebelled against God and were bound in the chains of that darkness until a future judgment would send them to their final punishment. Second Peter 2:4: "For if God spared not the angels that sinned, but cast them down to hell, and delivered them into chains of darkness, to be reserved unto judgment."

The beauty, brightness, and freshness of the creative works of this final day of creation opened to them the full manifestation of God's glory, power, grandeur, and love. They had not yet been given a single restriction, but had been told to replenish and subdue the earth "and have dominion over the fish of the sea, and the fowl of the air, and over every living thing that moveth upon the earth" (Genesis 1:28).

Amidst all of this grandeur, when God did give them one restriction, it did not seem to abate their delight, cause them concern, or question God as to why.

> And the Lord God commanded the man saying, Of every tree of the garden thou mayest freely eat. But of the tree of the knowledge of good and evil, thou shalt not eat of it; for in the day that thou eatest thereof thou shalt surely die.
>
> Genesis 2: 16–17

Only their Creator knew what the future held for them if they obeyed this one command. Only their Creator knew by whom they would be tempted, tested, and deceived into disobeying this command. Genesis 3:1 says, "Now the serpent was more subtil than any beast of the field which the Lord God had made." To reinforce the importance of obeying this one restriction, God introduced the judgment for disobeying. Genesis 2:16–17 says, "For in the day thou eatest thereof, thou shalt surely die." If man could resist this one temptation, and its tempter, the fullness of God's plans for man would eternally make this glorious setting their eternal home. However, amidst all of the beauty, grandeur, and peace of Eden, Adam and Eve would soon learn the awful results of disobedience. Their soul, spirit, and body would experience an awakened conscience to the corruption and guilt this evil would bring.

Satan, who is spirit, had taken possession of the serpent's body in order to approach God's new creation. In his spiritual form and nature, he had not yet had access to the human nature or being. This required his use of some visible form through which he could approach Eve, be seen by her, and communicate with her. Only through her would he have any opportunity to deceive and capture the crown of God's creation, and thereby gain access to the control of God's earthly creation. Satan knew God had given the power and authority over that creation only to Adam.

Satan did not allow Adam and Eve very long to enjoy the position into which God had placed them, nor long to enjoy the beauty and grandeur of all that surrounded them. What better time to make his attack than while Adam and Eve were just beginning to know God, to obey His commands and beginning to experience and exercise their authority over the earth and its creatures?

It is evident Satan had already been cast out of heaven and was silently and earnestly listening to and observing this renewal of the heaven and earth, and the new creation with which God was covering it. If he was going to have any chance to control this new creation and build his own kingdom on the earth, he had to wait to know whom to approach, what the approach should be, and when it should be made. How subtle Satan is. How deceitfully he works. How patient he can be, but how quickly he can act. How low he had fallen. He had once been a "prince of the most high God," but now he was only "the prince of the power of the air." How weak and empty that sounded. He would, through this new creation, seek to become the "god of this world." That sounded much loftier.

Satan's wisdom, prowess, cunning words, and ways were shown by his method of approach. He would be described as a "devourer," as a "roaring lion, seeking whom he may devour," but he was wise enough not to use those tactics for fear of scaring Eve directly to Adam and both of them running to God for protection. He would use the gentle approach, the spirit of an angel of light and the gentleness of a lamb, even though it would be done in the spirit of a wolf in sheep's clothing.

He would appear to Eve in a creature form she was already acquainted with and that Adam had already named. That combination made this creature "more subtil than any beast of the field which the Lord God had made" (Genesis 3:1). *Webster's Dictionary,* defines subtle as "marked by mental keenness, delicately skillful or clever, not open or direct, delicately suggestive, working insidiously and not easily detected." How fitting this is to the method, manner, and person of Satan as he approached Eve. Satan will use any of the names, forms, methods, or works identified as his to accomplish his goals with any individual.

Satan dared not approach Adam first and alone. He knew that only to Adam had God given the command not to eat from the "tree of the knowledge of good and evil," (Genesis 2:16–17). Eve did not hear this discourse because it took place just before God created her (verses 18, 21–24). Had he approached Adam first, Adam may have invoked the command of God as his reason for rejecting Satan's temptation. Once Satan had convinced Eve to eat, her state of innocence ended and she who had been the tempted became the tempter.

Satan may also have reasoned that since Adam was created in "the image and likeness" of God Himself, that godly nature within him would be stronger, wiser, and present greater resistance to him than Eve, who was created from a rib of Adam; and although Adam declared her to be bone of his bone and flesh of his flesh, she would be more susceptible to his subtlety and deceit than Adam.

We do not know why Eve was alone. Perhaps Satan had lured Adam away. Satan had enticed Eve to look at this tree and try to determine what made it different from all the other trees of the garden of Eden. Everything was so new Eve may never have given thought to this before. She was doing exactly what God's Word would later warn all of us about: "Abstain from all appearance of evil," (1 Thessalonians 5:22), and "Fear God, and keep His commandments" (Ecclesiastes 12:13).

Once Satan gets your attention, he has cunning ways, deceitful words, and logical reason so powerfully presented he would deceive the very elect if it were possible (Matthew 24:24).

We must also remember that Eve had never been confronted by Satan before, had not been warned about him, and only knew what Adam had told her God said to him about this tree and the results if they ate from it. Eve had never been tempted by evil before. She and Adam had only known good and had never been confronted with temptation; therefore, she was no match for Satan's deceitful logic. His logic had worked on the very angels of heaven, so why not on Eve?

There is a subtle warning to everyone in this account of the first sin. When God has banned something and sets a severe penalty on disobeying this ban, stay as far away from that thing as you can. Too many people have fallen victim to Satan's temptations by curiously examining something that is enticing but evil, or by trying to reason by the logic of man's senses why God has banned it.

Satan used a question to create doubt and pictured the quotation of Adam as illogical. Satan attempted to play ignorant and twisted God's words in order to create doubts and disbelief in Eve's mind.

Genesis 3:1: "And he said unto the woman, Yea, hath God said, Ye shall not eat of every tree of the garden?" He knew that God had not banned them from eating from all of the other trees, only this tree. Genesis 2:16: "And the Lord God commanded the man, saying, Of every tree of the garden thou mayest freely eat." Verse 17: "But of the tree of the knowledge of good and evil, thou shalt not eat of it."

Satan's exaggerated question engendered an exaggerated answer from Eve. Genesis 3:2–3: "And the woman said unto the serpent, We may eat of the fruit of the trees of the garden. But of the fruit of the tree which is in the midst of the garden, God hath said, Ye shall not eat of it, neither shall ye touch it, lest ye die." Her answer let Satan know she was playing right into his hands. God had not said, "Neither shall ye touch it," and the words, "lest ye die" are not as fearful as what God actually said, "Ye shall surely die."

Satan immediately recognized this subtle weakening in Eve and seized the moment. He would continue to mix some truth with a lie. This is the same tactic he still uses. An out and out lie is more easily recognized, questioned, and rejected than a lie mixed with some truth in order to achieve the desired results.

Satan challenges with, "Ye shall not surely die." This statement was a challenge to her trust in God's word, and also a direct challenge to God to fulfill the death sentence on "the day that thou eatest thereof."

Satan saw this as a win-win situation. If they ate and died that day, God lost the one source He had created to maintain control over the earth and its creation. If they ate from it and came under the death penalty, to be exercised at some point in the future, he would then become the winner.

To the eternal regret of all future generations of Adam and Eve, she weakened even further and looked longingly toward the tree and its fruit. That lingering look gave Satan the further opportunity to influence her thinking and change the course of her reasoning, "For God doth know that in the day ye eat thereof, then your eyes shall be opened, and ye shall be as gods, knowing good and evil" (Genesis 3:5).

Notice the cunning deceit mixed with partial truth. "Your eyes shall be opened." Eve had no concept of the truth of this statement or of the full meaning of it. She and Adam had only seen the glory, the liberty, the splendor, and the wonder of all that God had created around them and for them. Satan was subtly saying, "You haven't seen anything yet." In Eve's innocent mind, she began to reason, "If there is more, I want to see it, know it, and enjoy it."

The statement, "Your eyes shall be opened" created anticipation instead of striking fear in her heart, mind, and spirit. The anticipation of seeing more as God saw things overshadowed the warning of God, "thou shalt surely die." This was the initiation by Satan of the appeal to the flesh to enjoy the pleasures of the material world, which would turn to "the pleasures of sin for a season." This choice on her part to succumb to his lie would bring the death sentence to both she and Adam, and ultimately to all of their future generations, to all creatures about them, and make the place of their creation a vast burial ground for man and every creature. Because she would make this choice, hell would have to "enlarge herself to meet thee at thy coming" (Isaiah 5:14). Because of this choice, God's justice would demand a "white throne judgment," and all who come before it will be cast into the "lake of fire" with the fallen angels, the antichrist, the false prophet, and Satan, where they will be punished forever and ever (Revelation 20:11–15). Oh, what sad results for having opened before man what God had chosen to keep hidden.

Satan continued the enticement with, "And ye shall be as gods, knowing good and evil." Satan knew that God walked and talked with Adam and that Eve knew what great love and trust God had placed in them. She knew that it was to them He had offered the earth for them to subdue, all creatures for them to control, and every green herb for their meat. The concept Eve had of God was good. The very thought of His presence and the sound of His voice had thrilled both she and Adam. This was the only God she had known, and the thought of becoming more like Him struck a responsive cord in her mind, heart, and spirit. How and why should she resist becoming more like the God whom they knew? Satan made it seem almost an honorable thing rather than a horrible thing.

What Eve didn't know, couldn't conceive, and couldn't separate in her mind was the difference between the words *God* and *gods.* Satan made it sound honorable, respectful, and a challenge. How could she resist? Satan blinded her to the fact there is only one true and living God, Creator of heaven and earth, consisting of a Trinity, God the Father, God the Son, and God the Holy Ghost. What she did not know was that to be as gods would be in total opposition to the God she knew, would be in total rebellion against Him, and would be totally rejecting Him.

To be as gods would provide the open door through which Satan could take possession of man and bring him under his control and into Satan's warfare against God, their Creator. Those gods did not have the likeness and image of God as did Adam.

Satan's appeal to her humanity had succeeded. She was succumbing to the feelings of self-will. The spirit of independence was overcoming the spirit of dependence. The feeling of self-exaltation was beginning to awaken in her, and for the first time, she was feeling the need to be obeyed as a god, rather than obeying God as a servant and caretaker. For the first time, Satan was tempting her with the feeling of pride, which leads to a haughty spirit that leads to a fall. Proverbs 16:18 says, "Pride goeth before destruction and an haughty spirit before a fall."

Never had Eve been confronted with these different feelings. Never before had she any reason to question the restriction to the tree of the knowledge of good and evil. Never before had she been given the thought that she and Adam could become as gods. Never before had she any reason to believe this tree held the key to them becoming wiser than they were. Confronted by these new feelings and these new thoughts, she stared longingly at the forbidden tree.

Closely observing her mood, her words, and her actions, Satan quickly laid out before her three things that now appealed to her senses, her reasoning, and her pride. These three things would build her self-confidence, self-esteem, self-pride, thus awakening a carnal nature and stimulating a carnal desire. What worked on the innocent humanity in Eden has been used by Satan on humanity ever since. These three things are, "the lust of the flesh, the lust of the eye, and the pride of life." When these three things are presented to man by Satan, they can deaden man's spiritual nature and awaken his carnal nature. Satan still uses them successfully today.

> And when the woman saw that the tree was good
> for food, and that it was pleasant to the eyes, and
> a tree to be desired to make one wise, she took of
> the fruit thereof, and did eat, and gave also unto
> her husband with her; and he did eat.
>
> Genesis 3:6

Eve saw the forbidden fruit was good for food. This shows the fruit was appealing to the fleshly nature of Eve. When you can justify some fleshly good, what can be so evil about something? Why resist that which can provide benefits to this body?

"It was pleasant to the eyes." When Satan is subtly directing the scene before your eyes, he can cause you to look where you shouldn't look, see what you shouldn't see, and then justify that looking with the carnal feelings of fleshly pleasures that you shouldn't feel. When Eve had already been tempted with the fleshly desire to taste, the eye caused the forbidden fruit to begin to stir feelings of physical pleasure. Unless the Spirit and the Word intervene, the total concept of satisfying the flesh and enjoying the pleasures of life will not resist the final temptation, satisfying the ego by making it independent from all restrictions God has placed on how to live a life pleasing to Him.

Satan used this same approach and appeal on Jesus Christ in the wilderness temptation. If it had worked in Eden on the ones God had created in His image and likeness, Satan believed now was the time to try it on the Son of man, Jesus. As the Son of Man, He would be tempted in all points as man would be tempted (Hebrews 4:15). That temptation is recorded in Matthew 4:1–11.

Those three temptations came in the same manner, the same spirit, and from the same person who tempted Eve. Verse 1: "Then was Jesus led up of the spirit into the wilderness to be tempted of the devil." Jesus had just been baptized by John in the Jordan River. The Holy Spirit had descended as a dove and rested upon Him. His Father had just spoken from heaven confirming, "This is my beloved Son, in whom I am well pleased" (Matthew 3:13–17). Jesus prepared His body, mind, and spirit by fasting forty days and nights. Satan saw only the near exhaustion of the body from being without food for this time. He saw this self-denial as an opportunity, not as a barrier. Verse 2: "And when he had fasted forty days and forty nights, he was afterward an hungered." Satan recognized the weakness of the flesh without seeing the strength of the spirit. Read all of these verses in Matthew and see that Satan tempted Jesus with the same temptations he had succeeded with Eve. Each time, Jesus answered, "It is written." Eve only quoted God's word once. Jesus rejected Satan's appeals, but Eve began to look, think, and desire. Jesus successfully resisted Satan, but Eve succumbed.

Satan's words to her, "Your eyes shall be opened," created anticipation instead of warning. She ate of the forbidden fruit and then gave some to her husband, and "He did eat" (Genesis 3:6). They suddenly knew what changes come to the flesh when a carnal nature is awakened within it. Verse 7 says, "And the eyes of them both were opened, and they knew that they were naked; and they sewed fig leaves together, and made themselves aprons."

Though superior to every other creature God had created on the earth, in shame and burdened with guilt, they would be awakened to their own weakness, which had now become an imperfection. They would stand in horror and fear, when, for the first time with an awakened conscience, they heard God's voice speaking to them. For the first time in this sinful condition, the realization that they faced God's judgment of death caused them to attempt to hide from Him in fear and trembling (verse 8). For the first time they realized they could not hide from Him (verse 9). For the first time they realized they could not save themselves (verse 10). For the first time they realized what corruption of the body, soul, and spirit meant (verse 11). For the first time they realized who their enemy was and what he had done to them (verses 12–13). For the first time, man needed the mercy of God. He had experienced the love and favor of God, now he needed mercy.

They could repent of their sin and God could forgive them, but the seed of that sin would remain in them and be passed on to their heirs, beginning with their sons, Cain and Abel (Genesis 4:8).

This same seed of sin would then be passed to all of their future generations, causing us all to be sinners. Psalms 51:5 says, "Behold, I was shapen in iniquity; and in sin did my mother conceive me." Romans 5:12 says, "Wherefore, as by one man sin entered into the world, and death by sin; and so death passed upon all men, for that all have sinned."

This didn't happen without God's foreknowledge. Genesis 3:15 identifies God's plan of redemption. John 17:24–26, Matthew 25:34, and Hebrews 4:2–3 all confirm God had a plan of redemption before the foundation of the world. For that redemption to take place, God's justice must be satisfied. His judgment must be carried out and forgiveness with eternal cleansing must take place. Jesus Christ accomplished all of that for man.

God's First Action

God placed immediate judgment upon the serpent and then upon Satan. Genesis 3:14, unto the serpent God spoke:

> And the Lord God said unto the serpent, Because thou hast done this, thou art cursed above all cattle, and above every beast of the field; upon thy belly shalt thou go, and dust shalt thou eat all the days of thy life.

It is supposed the serpent had walked upright and had been one of the most beautiful and wisest of Earth's creatures prior to Satan entering him to tempt Eve. After that temptation had caused Eve and then Adam to sin, God cursed him above all other creatures, causing him to crawl on his belly, and by crawling upon his belly, everything he ate would be tainted by the dust from which Adam and

Eve were made. He would never be free from the results of that for which Satan had used him. Every bite of dust-tainted food would be the symbol of why God's judgment had placed him upon his belly on the ground.

God clearly identifies the person to whom this is spoken, the reason why it is spoken, and the degree of judgment this action would bring. "And the Lord God said unto the serpent," identifies to whom this is spoken. "Because thou hast done this," states the reason for God's action. "Thou art cursed above all cattle, and above every beast of the field," is the degree of judgment. "Upon thy belly shalt thou go, and dust shalt thou eat all the days of thy life," removes any hope of changing the conditions of this judgment for the serpent. This evidentiary record of the serpent's actions would stand eternally as justification for the threefold judgment God would carry out upon the serpent.

Notice (1) How swiftly it came. The serpent was asked no questions and was not given an opportunity to defend himself or his actions, nor to place blame on Satan. (2) He immediately stood condemned. "Because thou hast done this," declared his guilt by his actions. (3) The absolute authority by which it was pronounced. Only God the Creator has the omnipresence, omniscience, and omnipotence that would justify the absolute authority by which this sentence was pronounced and carried out.

It appears this is the time God also placed a curse upon the other creatures. "Thou art cursed above the cattle, and above every beast of the field." This is not mentioned again in the Scripture, but its effects remain upon all of these creatures and the earth. It will not be removed until it becomes the final act of cleansing for the earth and all creatures affected by it. Revelation 22:3: "And there shall be no more curse."

God's Second Action

Genesis 3:15, God spoke to Satan, "And I will put enmity between thee and the woman, and between thy seed and her seed: it shall bruise thy head, and thou shalt bruise his heel." It is clear that these words, though directed to the serpent, were being directed to Satan, who had taken possession of the serpent's body.

This verse was God's promise of a Redeemer for man and an eternal defeat for Satan. This referred to Jesus Christ, the war between Him and Satan over man, and what God had given man to possess.

Satan, who was spirit, had taken possession of the body of the serpent in order to approach this new creation of God. In his spiritual form, he had not yet had access to the man or woman. This required his use of some visible form through which he could approach Eve, be seen by her, and communicate with her. Only then did he have any opportunity to deceive and capture these who were the crown of this creation of God.

"Between thy seed and her seed" is important to understand. To whom was God referring by using the words *thy seed?* It must refer to those individuals who allow Satan to take possession of them, who are possessed of that spirit of independence, which was the basic spirit that created the great chasm between Lucifer and God. It was this spirit that brought about the fall of many other angels whom Lucifer deceived, and had now caused the fall of man.

It was this spirit that caused the first conflict between Cain and Abel, the two sons of Adam and Eve. John identifies it in I John 3:12, when he declares that, "Cain was of that wicked one, and slew his brother." Why did he slay his brother? "Because his own works were evil and his brother's righteous." This presents the picture of this enmity in its first activity. Cain was here identified as being "of that wicked one," and Abel was identified as being "righteous."

It was against the "seed of Satan" Jesus directed His words in Matthew 12:34: "O generation of vipers, how can ye being evil speak good things?" He also traces the works of Satan that were the "bruising of the heel" of the seed of the woman (Matthew 23:13–36), and pronounces eight woes upon the scribes and Pharisees and hypocrites all the way down from righteous Abel unto the blood of Zacharias, son of Barachias, "Whom ye slew between the temple and the altar," verse 35. These are the works of the "seed of Satan" against the "seed of the woman," and they continue yet today.

It was this spirit of independence in the scribes and Pharisees against Jesus Christ, God's redeemer to man, that caused Jesus to declare them to be "of your father the Devil" (John 8:44). This clearly identifies Satan's seed as being unregenerate man. They have blindly believed the lie of Satan, become his children by inheritance and choice, and will ultimately receive the same judgment of eternal containment and suffering in the lake of fire with Satan, the antichrist, and the false prophet.

Who is this seed of the woman? What we identified as the seed of Satan cannot refer to the entire human race. Man, in general, is almost always referred to as the seed of Adam and Eve. In Genesis 3:15, the seed of the woman is referred to as a single person to battle Satan; "It shall bruise thy head, and thou shalt bruise his heel."

This makes much clearer who the seed of the woman is, since man cannot redeem himself and neither can he successfully fight Satan alone. The only one to whom this can refer must be Jesus Christ. His virgin birth makes Him the only person ever born who was not of the seed of man.

> Now the birth of Jesus Christ was on this wise; When as his mother Mary was espoused to Joseph; before they came together, she was found with child of the Holy Ghost.
>
> Matthew 1:18

> But while he thought on these things, behold, the angel of the Lord appeared unto him in a dream, saying, Joseph, thou son of David, fear not to take unto thee Mary thy wife: for that which is conceived in her is of the Holy Ghost. And she shall bring forth a son, and thou shalt call his name JESUS: for he shall save his people from their sins.
>
> Matthew 1:20–21

This is the same virgin and son referred to in Isaiah 7:14: "Therefore, the Lord himself shall give you a sign; Behold, a virgin shall conceive, and bear a son, and shall call his name Immanuel."

It is the continuation of this conflict that will bring the tribulation and Armageddon, ending the kingdom of Satan among men, and bring to a close what is referred to in Luke 21:24 as "the times of the Gentiles be fulfilled." "And they shall fall by the edge of the sword, and shall be led away captive into all nations: and Jerusalem shall be trodden down of the Gentiles, until the times of the Gentiles be fulfilled" Luke 21:24.

It is also this conflict that shall come to a final end at the close of the millennial reign of Jesus Christ, after Satan has been loosed for a little season from the bottomless pit and goes out to deceive the nations that are in the four quarters of the earth (Revelation 20:7–9). Verse 10 declares the seed of the woman, Jesus Christ, wins this battle and becomes the eternal victor. "And the devil that deceived them was cast into the lake of fire and brimstone where the beast and false prophet are, and shall be tormented day and night, for ever and ever." This deals the eternal deathblow to Satan and all of his followers.

In spite of this hope of redemption for man, God's justice demanded His judgment be carried out upon the man and the woman.

God's Third Action

This verse declares God's judgments upon the woman:

> Unto the woman he said, I will greatly multiply thy sorrow and thy conception; in sorrow thou shalt bring forth children; and thy desire shall be to thy husband, and he shall rule over thee.
>
> Genesis 3:16

This judgment deals with three areas of her life: (1) conception, (2) birth of children, and (3) relationship to her husband.

From the time of conception up to the time of birth, many are the pains, the sorrows, and the complications that can be experienced by the woman. Beginning with conception, from early mornings and throughout the days as the time of birth nears, her pains may increase and her complications may change until her sorrows culminate in the pains of the birth of her child. She can rejoice as the child is delivered into her arms, but what she has experienced from conception to birth is the judgment of God for Eve having yielded to Satan's temptations in the Garden of Eden.

"And thy desire shall be to thy husband, and he shall rule over thee," returns her to the point of her beginning. This establishes a rule of physical relationship between Adam and Eve that reflects a rule of spiritual relationship between Christ and His church.

> Wives, submit yourselves unto your own husbands, as unto the Lord. For the husband is the head of the wife, even as Christ is the head of the Church: and he is the saviour of the body. Therefore as the Church is subject unto Christ, so let the wives be to their own husbands in every thing.
>
> Ephesians 5:22–24

This is also referred to in 1 Timothy 2:9–15. The husband's relationship and responsibility to his wife is in Ephesians 5:25–33.

God's Fourth Action

Adam attempted to cover his sin by putting the blame first on God, Genesis 3:12, "And the man said, the woman whom thou gavest to be with me," and then on Eve, "She gave me of the tree and I did eat." God then places the blame, guilt, and judgment on Adam for doing what he had just admitted.

Genesis 3:17–19 declares God's judgments upon the man:

> And unto Adam he said, Because thou hast hearkened unto the voice of thy wife, and hast eaten of the tree, of which I commanded thee, saying, Thou shalt not eat of it: cursed is the ground for thy sake; in sorrow shalt thou eat of it all the days of thy life. Thorns also and thistles shall it bring forth to thee; and thou shalt eat the herb of the field. In the sweat of thy face shalt thou eat bread, till thou return unto the ground; for out of it wast thou taken: for dust thou art, and unto dust shalt thou return.

The blame, guilt, and judgment upon the serpent, Satan, and Eve was direct and personal, but upon Adam, it was first personal and then extended to the earth and all that God had given him control over. This destroys the theory of many who teach the inherent evil of all matter. They have it backward. God Himself declared that all He had created was very good (Genesis 1:31). Evil and its results did not begin in the earth and then transfer to Adam. The earth was cursed because of the sin of Adam. It continues to groan under that curse for his sin. Romans 8:22 says, "For we know that the whole creation groaneth and travaileth in pain together until now." Verse 23 affirms that the effects of the curse extend even to those who are redeemed:

> And not only they, but ourselves also, which have the firstfruits of the Spirit, even we ourselves groan within ourselves, waiting for the adoption, to wit, the redemption of our body.

It is not until all other results, effects, and judgments for sin have been removed that the earth is finally and eternally relieved and cleansed of this curse. Revelation 22:3 says, "And there shall be no more curse." The crown of thorns Jesus wore on the cross was representative of His suffering the judgment of God for the sin of Adam, and one day, that curse will be removed.

God would also drive Adam and Eve from the Garden of Eden, denying them access to the tree of life, thus preventing them from eating from it and living forever in that sinful state. Man will not have access to it again until he is in a glorified state, in the heavenly New Jerusalem.

> And in the midst of the street of it, and on either side of the river, was there the tree of life, which bare twelve manner of fruits, and yielded her fruit every month, and the leaves of the tree were for the healing of the nations.
>
> Revelation 22:2

Driving them from Eden satisfied the justice of God while they were living, and it also satisfied the justice of God by enforcing the penalty of death. Only by His love, mercy, and grace will He give man access to it again, and that will be in the New Jerusalem.

What a sad portrait of man this presents, after having seen his glorious beginning before Satan entered the scene. Along with man, the eternal future for all of the earthly creation was changed, and only because of Genesis 3:15 was there any hope of some means and degree of restoration. Thank God, He made and will fulfill that provision.

The Establishment of Families

The union of male and female was God's plan for establishing families upon the earth, and through these families, they would "be fruitful and multiply and replenish the earth" (Genesis 1:28). This meant that Adam and Eve would bear children, their children would bear children, and this would continue until the purpose and plan of God for man was fulfilled.

This began in Genesis 4:1: "And Adam knew Eve his wife; and she conceived, and bare Cain, and said, I have gotten a man from the Lord." The family grew. Verse 2: "And she again bare his brother Abel. And Abel was a keeper of sheep, but Cain was a tiller of the ground." This reveals the individual characteristics of these two sons, and these individual characteristics would reflect the beginning of diversity in their future generations. It would also reflect their differences in respect to God's favor and their spiritual relationship to Him.

Verses 3–16 provide a picture of this first family's inherited sinful nature and the spiritual, physical, moral problems and conflicts created by that sinful nature.

We are not given an account of the birth of the first females, but it appears to have happened before Eve bore another son. Genesis 4:17: "And Cain knew his wife; and she conceived, and bare Enoch: and he builded a city, and called the name of the city after the name of his son, Enoch." This clearly gives evidence of females having been born, families developing, and the population spreading, shown by the building of this first city.

Verses 17–24 give a genealogic account of the family of Cain. The sinful nature he inherited from his father Adam continued and was passed on to his children. Lamech told his two wives he had killed two men. We are also given a picture of the great diversity of their interests, talents, and skills, which included farming and ranching, becoming musicians, and working in brass and iron.

Verse 25 then gives the record of Adam and Eve's third son, Seth. "And Adam knew his wife again; and she bare a son, and called his name Seth: for God, said she, hath appointed me another seed instead of Abel, whom Cain slew." Seth had a son, and the diversity of Adam and Eve's family, their talents and skills, continued to grow.

It appears Cain did not influence his family religiously but left with them a continuing record of conflict, evil, and murder. Seth was God's replacement of righteous Abel, and family worship began with Seth's family, after the birth of his first son, Enos, in verse 26: "then began men to call upon the name of the Lord."

From that point on, families began to rapidly increase upon the earth—Genesis 5:1 says, "This is the book of the generations of Adam"—and they are listed through Noah. It is continued in chapter 6:

> And it came to pass, when men began to multiply on the face of the earth, and daughters were born unto them. That the sons of God saw the daughters of men that they were fair; and they took them wives of all which they chose.

So many conjectures surround the meaning of the phrase "the sons of God saw the daughters of men." Who are the sons of God and the daughters of men? I believe this simply reflects God's creative process. God created man from the dust of the earth in His own likeness and His own image and then created the woman from the man. This clearly identifies why the sons are called the sons of God and why the daughters are called the daughters of men.

I don't believe these sons of God can be angels, because angels are neither male nor female, even though archangels have male names. God never intended them to increase or replace the angels that fell with Lucifer. Angels are spirits without mortal bodies; therefore, they could not marry and produce children with the daughters of men.

The Bible calls all believers children of God.

> You are all the children of God through faith in Christ Jesus. For as many of you as have been baptized into Christ put on Christ. There is neither Jew nor Greek, bond nor free, there is neither male nor female: for ye are all one in Christ Jesus.
>
> Galatians 3:26–28

The next verse then ties all of this new spiritual relationship and nature through Jesus Christ together with that of the Old Testament faith, family, and nature of Abraham. Verse 29 says, "And if ye be Christ's, then are ye Abraham's seed, and heirs according to the promise."

"If ye be Christ's" clearly refers to the spiritual birth and spiritual relationship, not to the physical genetic or biological relationship. In the physical genetic relationship, there is yet Jew and Gentile even after having accepted Jesus Christ. This verse also provides the spiritual genealogical relationship of the Old and New Testament saints.

Diversity with the Families

Beginning with the first family, and continuing through succeeding generations, we see the great diversity in their interests, talents, standards, desires, thoughts, morals, and actions. This great diversity among children from the same original genetic parents, Adam and Eve, and the biological generations that followed them, reflect the omniscience of God and the futuristic planning, purposes, and works of God that He invested in man.

First

When we think of the magnitude, the manifold potentials, and the mystery of the marvelous endowments, and yet with the great diversity God created within each man, it boggles the mind. The Psalmist described it in the most Godly of terms when he said, "I will praise thee; for I am fearfully and wonderfully made: marvelous are thy works; and that my soul knoweth right well" (Psalms 139:14).

When God created the earth, He poured its entire potential into it. The future development of its mysteries, marvels, hidden treasures, unlimited resources, boundless combinations, interrelationships, and unthinkable discoveries will never be exhausted. Each succeeding generation continues to unlock, unravel, identify, discover, and develop the magnitude of these endowments and the potential of all of these resources. By this, man continues to reveal the magnitude, marvel, and mystery of the creative wisdom, power, and presence that God has invested in all of His creation. It is because of this man will keep discovering, developing, and increasing the potential of every area of life, every area of nature, and every area of the land, sea, and air. Because of the omniscience, omnipotence, and omnipresence of God, this will continue for eternity.

Second

God invested in man the one potential to accomplish this when He said:

> Let us make man in our image, after our likeness: and let them have dominion over the fish of the sea, and over the fowl of the air, and over the cattle, and over all the earth, and over every creeping thing that creepeth upon the earth. So God created man in his own image, in the image of God created he him; male and female created he them.
>
> Genesis 1:26–27

God knew that man was going to be the possessor, overseer, and developer of all that He was creating in, upon, and above the earth and its two heavens; therefore, in the creative process, He endowed man with all of the requirements to guarantee that man's potential, talents, wisdom, and powers would never be surpassed by any other creature of this creation nor from the heavenly creation. Man can build worldly kingdoms, but those will fall. Satan has intruded, attempting to build his kingdom, but he will never take ultimate and eternal possession or control.

This endowment would forever establish within the potential of man, the inherent nature, knowledge, wisdom, understanding, talent, ability, power, desires, thoughts, and actions to bring to fruition all that God has creatively hidden within the earth and its two heavens. It is the continual development of these aspects of man that has caused some to believe in the theory of evolution instead of the theory of divine creation.

Because of God's act of creating man in His own image and likeness, and giving him dominion over all the earth, Jesus could rebuke and reject the three offers of Satan in the wilderness temptation simply by saying, "It is written" (Luke 4:1–13). Satan wanted Jesus to believe he could fulfill all he was tempting Him with, but Jesus knew God had already decreed man's rights to it, and He also knew what its potential was for man. "But as it is written, eye hath not seen, nor ear heard, neither have entered into the heart of man, the things which God hath prepared for them that love him" (1 Corinthians 2:9). In the proceeding verses, Paul reveals how these things will come to man. "What man can see, know, and prophesy is now only in part, but there is coming a time when that which is in part shall be done away, then we shall have revealed to us and can then understand and experience all that God has prepared for us" (1 Corinthians 13:9–12).

Just as God had system and order in the creative process developing each part of creation to complement, supply, support, and sustain the creation of the next day, so He has designed, endowed, and will unlock all of the creative mysteries, marvels, and potentials into realities as each generation progresses and passes, and "Of the increase of his government and peace there shall be no end, upon the throne of David, and upon his kingdom, to order it, and to establish it with judgment and with justice from henceforth even for ever. The zeal of the Lord of hosts will perform this" (Isaiah 9:7).

The potential of both man and all of the rest of creation is still in its infancy. The progress in man's wisdom, knowledge, understanding, talents, and developments of what God has invested in every area of creation for him is no more than a millisecond of what shall be revealed, developed, and come to reality in the eternal future as God opens it all to men.

The Psalmist declared, "marvelous are thy works" (Psalms 139:14). Paul confirmed it. "His ways are past finding out" (Romans 11:33). We can delve into them, search and research them, design and develop them, explore and expand them, but each progressive step only whets the appetite to see the next discovery and creates excitement when man realizes his most advanced knowledge and achievements are nothing more than the most simplistic, the most elemental, and the briefest of all that lies ahead.

In the present mind and body of this life, we are limited by the mortal ability to only see in part and know in part. What one generation sees, discovers, and develops often becomes passé and outdated, even considered obsolete or ancient while they are yet living. Younger minds will build upon, expand, create, and develop what may not have even been within the dream power or the imagination level of the previous generation, even while that generation might still be living.

This increase is only limited to and by the imperfections of man's present status, but how wonderful are the glorious things that shall become realities when this earth and man have been liberated from the power, influence, restraints, and deceitfulness of sin, Satan, and the curse. How marvelous when sin's restraints on the mind, body, and soul are gone from the mortals who inherit the earth to inhabit it for eternity. Each individual will eternally add to man's accumulated knowledge, wisdom, understanding, and experience. Unhindered by previous limitations, they will be expanding their growth into all the ways, works, and wonders of God that have been reserved from all who live with the restraints of this present mortality. First Corinthians 13:9–10 says, "For we know in part, and we prophesy in part. But when that which is perfect is come, that which is in part shall be done away."

Third

Read Genesis 5 and 6 regarding the generations of Adam, and see the great diversity that came into the family of man within those first few generations. Think of the slow development of the level of that diversity from Adam to only a few hundred years ago and then look at it today. Finally, recall the prophecy of the last days. Daniel 12:4 says, "But thou, O Daniel, shut up the words, and seal the book, even to the time of the end: many shall run to and fro, and knowledge shall be increased." A brief look at this instruction to Daniel, and what has taken place within the past two hundred years, will quickly show we are living in the time of the end. Until two hundred years ago, travel was no better or faster than it was in Daniel's time. Until two hundred years ago, communication was little faster than it was in Daniel's time. Until two hundred years ago, the increase of knowledge was little faster than it was in Daniel's time. Look at it today. All of this gives evidence we are living in the time of the end.

We live in an explosive world. An explosion of population, knowledge, inventions, discoveries, wars, corruption, mistrust, deceit, and every conceivable type of sin has taken place. There has been an explosion of technology, communication, transportation, and mechanization. We have seen an explosion of the sciences, including medical science, chemistry, biology, astrology, astronomy, and on we could go into every area of life and then realize we are still living in the infancy of all of these areas.

Regardless of all of these increases, we are yet living in the time when man only knows in part and sees in part. We are living while man and creation are still burdened under the imperfections created by the sinful fall of man, while yet under the curse upon the earth, and while we are yet fighting the powers and works of Satan to defeat God's cause, purpose, plan, provisions, and promises of manifesting the potential of His creative works through man.

Oh, how great the potential is for all creation when "that which is in part shall be done away," and the revelation of the wonders God has reserved for man become a part of everyday life. First Corinthians 3:19 says, "For the wisdom of this world is foolishness with God." What wonders are yet to be revealed.

The Development of Civilization

Civilization did not come into being through a process of evolution alone, but has evolved into its many different stages, forms, and cultures as a result of its creation, its nature, and purpose through the creative gifts and works of God's divine plan.

Civilization can be described as the civil development, organization, and administration of the cultural, social, intellectual, political, economic, religious, and family relationships of man. Each of these are identified separately by the things they produce in the life of man. Let's look briefly at some of them individually.

First: Cultural

This is the development, training and refinement of the mind, emotions, interests, manners, tastes, skills, and actions that reflect man's interaction with man through outside things God had created, but that man has refined, developed, and merged into his humanistic standards.

Second: Social

This is the ability for human beings to live together as a group, in a situation or environment in which their interactions with one another affects their common welfare, developing group friendships, establishing individual companionships, and offering assistance, fellowship, and various services as may be needed within a group or groups.

Third: Intellectual

This is the ability to receive into the mind, through any of man's senses, information in many forms from diverse resources and then analyze this information, interpret it, and translate that information into perception, knowledge, thoughts, reason, wisdom, and understanding. Once it is stored in the mind, it can then be retrieved, shared, and applied in whatever manner best suits man's purpose and use of that information. This then is transferred from the mind into relationships, judgments, interests, influences, and actions by the individual or within the group.

Fourth: Political

Theoretically, this is the development of a system by which individuals or all human units can be peacefully and profitably merged, controlled, and governed, granting rights and privileges or prohibiting unjust treatment by the few or by many and carrying out all privileges, needs, benefits, welfare, and interests that is intended for the betterment of all within that group.

Fifth: Economic

This is the development, management, distribution, and expenditure of wealth and other resources that have material and physical value to satisfactorily meet the needs, desires, purposes, and values of families, businesses, institutions, communities, and governments.

Sixth: Religion

To most, this is the belief in a divine, supreme, superhuman person, power, and government, providing a person, system, belief, and worship through which the individual has a specific set of standards and code of ethics that governs their personal life. From this, they develop a philosophy that governs their personal beliefs, practices, worship, and relationships. This spiritual power can then control, direct, punish, reward, curse, or bless their lives as they adhere to their faith, loyalty, and service for the honor, satisfaction, pleasure, and glory of that supreme being.

Seventh: Family

The family is a specific social, physical, and spiritual unit that, by marriage, consists of parents and children becoming one household. In a more general sense, it extends to biological relatives of both parents, as well as those related by marriage, including those who will become a part of the general family unit and as future descendents of a specific family unit. We believe it was initiated by God on earth as a reflection of what God Himself had already established in heaven. For this reason, the Scriptures makes reference to "the whole family of God." Ephesians 3:14–15: "For this cause I bow my knees unto the Father of our Lord Jesus Christ. Of whom the whole family in heaven and earth is named."

These are some of the basics that provide evidence that a divine Creator, and not simply an earthly force of evolution, provided the initial plans, resources, power, wisdom, and guidance to coordinate, develop, and blend all of these into the myriads of individual lives with both literal, physical, and mystical spiritual unions.

Only a divine mind could conceive, plan, and give purpose to what we know as civilization. Only divine power could produce the elements, resources, and beings of such a civilization. Only a divine person can direct, control, enjoy, and reward or destroy such a civilization. That mind, power, and person is the Lord God almighty, the Triune God. It was only after the Triune God had created all things within the heavens and the earth that there was any possibility that an evolutionary process, either natural or manmade, could have any developmental effect upon anything He had created. This evolutionary process could only proceed by drawing upon those things God had already purposely endowed within His creation. That process continues today as man continually unlocks and develops what this creation holds. Only in this manner can we as Christian believers accept an evolutionary process as being a part of the plan and purpose God had when He so freely endowed man with the many gifts, resources, and potential wisdom, knowledge, and understanding to develop what He had so lavishly bestowed at the time of creation, as recorded in Genesis 1.

Tribes Were Developed

Biblically, the words *tribe* and *tribes* have been reserved exclusively for the children of Israel, the descendants of Abraham.

Beginning in Genesis 49:16 and 28 to its last usage in Revelation 22:12, not one time does it refer to those who were not of the lineage of Abraham, the children of Israel. The word *tribe* is used 235 times, and the word *tribes* appears 111 times, all related to Israel. This means that throughout the biblically recorded history of man, the words *tribe* or *tribes* belongs exclusively to Israel.

Why? It could be that God knew these people would be scattered among all nations of the earth for many generations, but there would come a time when He would gather them together again and restore them to their promised homeland.

There would also become what is known as the ten lost tribes of Israel. They may be lost to man, having become scattered around the globe and integrated into other nations, which could bring different genealogical characteristics, colors, or national traits, but they are known to God, and he has preserved their individual tribal identity, tracked their every footstep, mapped their every homeland, and when Revelation 21:24–27 is fulfilled, not one of any of the twelve tribes of Israel shall be lost to God.

A brief look at many of the nations of the world will find several whose early population had been describes as tribes. Examples of this can be found in Africa, North America, Australia, and some other areas. This does not conflict with the biblical account. Who knows but what they are a part of the ten lost tribes, and God has used the word *tribe* as His means of not loosing their genealogical identity in His records, even though they may remain unidentified by the records of man. There will come a time when God brings all twelve tribes together. As assurance this will happen, all we have to do is trust in the God of Israel, who was omnipresent when the scattering took place, who is omniscient and knows where they have been and where they are now, and who is omnipotent, having all power to bring them together again and restore everything that will fulfill His covenant to Abraham.

By reserving the words *tribe* and *tribes* exclusively for the children of Israel, their identity could be established regardless of what land and what people they had been scattered within, and they could be separated from all other families, cities, or nations of people.

Tribes are distinctly separated from tongues, people, and nations. Before God separated Abraham and his generations from other people, these words referred to everyone, but revealed distinctions. Genesis 10:20 says, "These are sons of Ham, after their families, after their tongues, in their countries, and in their nations." Genesis 10:31 says, "These are the sons of Shem, after their families, after their tongues, in their lands, after their nations." Verse 32 says, "These are the families of the sons of Noah, after their generations, in their nations, and by these were the nations divided in the earth after the flood.

The word *tongues* refers to their family dialects and was used as a means of individual family identity. This was before Babel, and the "whole earth was of one language, and of one speech" (Genesis 11:1). Therefore, the word *tongues* could not yet mean different languages or speech. At this time, families were classified or identified genetically by their specific forefathers and their bloodlines.

The word *people* is first used when God looked upon those who had come to the land of Shinar. Genesis 11:6 says, "And the Lord said, Behold, the people is one, and they have all one language; and this they begin to do: and now nothing will be restrained from them, which they have imagined to do." The word *people* was here expanded from one genetically related family, Cush, to a gathering of people who were building cities, from which they would have identities related to their cities. Genesis 10:10 says, "And the beginning of his kingdom was Babel, and Eriech, and Accad, and Calneh, in the land of Shinar." Even though God recognized them as one, referring to their unified intent on building "a city and a tower, whose top may reach unto heaven; and let us make us a name, lest we be scattered abroad upon the face of the whole earth" (verse 4), they were also beginning to develop and identify with their blended families, bloodlines, and homelands. They had greatly increased in numbers and had begun marrying outside of their individual family members, but still within their genetic lineage. These were from Cush.

The word *nation* or *nations* identifies people by geographical, political, and governmental boundaries and was used by God in His covenant with Abraham. The use of the word *tribe* would retain Israel's genetic identity from that of other *people,* families, or nations, but in contrast, clearly and purposely keeps them separate without specifically calling them Israel. Later, all of the tribes of Israel would be identified as the *nation of Israel* and would be given a specific homeland, keeping God's promise in His covenant with Abraham, and in keeping with the meaning of the word *nation.* "I will make of thee a great nation" (Genesis 12:2). God also promised Abraham, "Of the bondwoman will I make a nation" (Genesis 21:13). This referred to Ishmael and his descendants.

It is interesting to note that before God called Abraham and established his generations through Isaac, Sarah's son, God did not use the word *tribe* or *tribes* when identifying genetical and genealogical lines of descendants from Adam (Genesis 5:1–32), nor in identifying the genetical and genealogical lines of descendants from Noah after the flood (Genesis 10:1–32). This further confirms its use was restricted to the generations of Abraham.

Matthew 24:29–31:

> Immediately after the tribulation of those days shall the sun be darkened, and the moon shall not give her light, and the stars shall fall from heaven, and the powers of the heavens shall be shaken. And then shall appear the sign of the Son of man in heaven: and then shall all the tribes of the earth mourn, and they shall see the Son of man coming in the clouds of heaven with power and great glory. And he shall send his angels with a great sound of a trumpet, and they shall gather together his elect from the four winds, from one end of heaven to the other.

This is after the tribulation and after Armageddon. It is after the time of the Gentiles has been fulfilled. It is after the destruction of the Gentile armies of the earth, after the fowls have drunk their blood and devoured their flesh. It is after the greatest earthquake the world has known and will ever know, when all the cities of the nations (except Jerusalem, which shall be divided) will have been destroyed, and the remnant not destroyed during the tribulation or at Armageddon shall be destroyed. Thus, those who are referred to are not Gentiles.

In these verses, it is clear the word *tribes* refers to Israel, because He gathers His elect from the four winds, from one end of heaven to the other. The word *elect* determines this is Israel. This is after the Gentile nations are gone, when God brings all of the tribes of Israel together, introducing them to Jesus Christ, the Son of man, and when Israel will, as a nation, accept Jesus Christ as their Messiah, and they shall be His people, and He shall be their God (Revelation 21:3–8).

The Development of Cities and Nations

From the families of the sons of Adam and Eve, Cain and Seth, the unity of families revealed itself almost immediately. To have done so this early in man's history means that God must have built into the body, mind, and spirit of man a sense of physical, emotional, and spiritual unity and relationship that was not learned but was inherent and only needed nurturing and expression. This same spirit of family unity and relationship is seen to some degree within all living creatures. This reflects a relationship of all creatures to God, who created all things as a part of His family.

The fact that God established the marriage relationship to require the persons to leave father and mother, and be joined to one another as one flesh, did not weaken this unity, but strengthened and expanded it to succeeding generations. As each family unit developed and expanded, those family bonds kept the units close together, and beginning with Cain and his children, cities began to be formed. Genesis 4:17 says, "And Cain knew his wife; and she conceived, and bare Enoch: and he builded a city, and called the name of the city, after the name of his son, Enoch."

Notice the reflection of this close family spirit. "And he called the name of the city, after the name of his son, Enoch." That reflects not only the unity and relationship of this family, but also the love and pride that existed within it. This is especially significant from the fact that it was this Cain who earlier had slain his brother Abel (Genesis 4:8). It is also significant from the fact that Cain was driven from his home because of this. Verse 16 says, "And Cain went out from the presence of the Lord, and dwelt in the land of Nod, on the east of Eden." This shows that family unity, relationship, and love can and does exist, not just within the spiritual part of man but also within the physical, mortal nature of man. From Cain on, as family units developed, so did cities.

The tenth chapter of Genesis presents the first picture and description of nations. Families had flourished and were spreading across the earth. As this happened, they began settling the lands and used different means of identifying boundaries and developing government as they began to fulfill God's purpose for Adam and Eve.

Genesis 1:26 says,

> And God said, Let us make man in our image, after our likeness: and let them have dominion over the fish of the sea, and over the fowl of the air, and over the cattle, and over all the earth, and over every creeping thing that creepeth upon the earth.

As Adam and Eve began to fulfill the command of God to "be fruitful, and multiply, and replenish the earth" (Genesis 1:28), the population increased rapidly. Nations began to form, producing leaders who developed governance, protective services, social traits, and moral practices after those of their leaders.

As these nations grew, their people would develop specific skills, talents, lifestyles, and living habits suitable to that people. This was briefly referred to in the discussion of the "Diversity within Families." Genesis chapters 5 and 6 present the earliest discussion of this diversity. Genesis 5:1 introduces it as the "book of the generations of Adam."

As the family units of the sons of Noah developed after the flood, so did cities, kingdoms, and nations. Genesis 10:5 says, "By these were the isles of the Gentiles divided in their lands; every one after his tongue, after their families, in their nations." These were the families of the sons of Japheth. Genesis 10:11–12 shows us the beginning of the cities, nations, and kingdoms, through the sons of Ham:

> And the beginning of his kingdom was Babel, and Erech, and Accad, and Calneh, in the land of Shinar. Out of that land went forth Asshur, and builded Nineveh, and the city Rehoboth, and Calah. And Resen between Nineveh and Calah: the same is a great city.

From Genesis 10:21–31, we trace the families of Shem and their dwelling from "Mesha, as thou goest unto Sephar a mount of the east." From this beginning, after the flood, all cities and nations have developed.

There are two specific cities that have a particular place in history and prophecy: Babylon, representative of corruption and evil, and Jerusalem, representative of righteousness and the city of God on earth. Revelation 17 presents the destruction of the evil spiritual Babylon, and chapter 18 presents the destruction of the wicked commercial Babylon.

The individual families that made up the *tribes* of Israel together make up the *nation* of Israel. That people and nation stands separate from all others and are the focus of much of the events of the last days. Its capital, Jerusalem, will become the only city left standing when the holocaust of Armageddon is over, and will be there as the holy city referred to at the end of the millennial reign of Jesus Christ. Revelation 20:9 says, "And they went up on the breadth of the earth, and compassed the camp of the saints about, and the beloved city: and fire came down from

God out of heaven, and devoured them." When this cleansing by fire is completed, and the judgments of the white throne judgment is fulfilled (Revelation 20:11–15), and the curse is removed from the earth (Revelation 22:3), nothing shall hinder or prohibit the fulfillment of the Lord's Prayer. "Thy kingdom come. Thy will be done in earth, as it is in heaven."

From this time on, all tribes, cities, kingdoms, and nations shall belong to Jesus Christ, and over them, He and His Bride shall rule and reign forever and ever.

God Declares His Disappointment with Man

As generations multiplied and civilization developed, this seed of sin became so overpowering that when God looked down upon the earth, He saw the horrible condition of man.

Genesis 6:5-6 says,

> And God saw that the wickedness of man was great in the earth, and that every imagination of the thoughts of his heart was only evil continually. And it repented the Lord that he had made man on the earth, and it grieved him at his heart.

Think of all God had created, with all of its potential benefits for man's future home, happiness, and blessing, and within such a short time, He repents that He had even made man. The very nature of God Himself was affected by what He saw, and "it grieved him at his heart." How sadly this reflects back upon the exciting words God had spoken when He declared He would create man in His own image and His own likeness (Genesis 1:26). Think how bold His plans for man were when He gave him the rights over all the earth and its creatures. He trusted man when He told him he could eat from every tree in the garden except the tree of the knowledge of good and evil (Genesis 2:18). This soon changed from a scene of blessing to one of eternal judgment and separation from all God had planned and provided to man.

God drove man from Eden and sealed it so man could never have access to the fruit of the tree of life until after He had provided a means of restoring man spiritually, through the new birth in Christ Jesus, and physically, through His stripes.

The fruit of the tree of life does not restore or give life, but would provide the nourishment to sustain life.

Genesis 3:22–24:

> And the Lord God said, Behold, the man is become as one of us, to know good and evil; and now, lest he put forth his hand, and take also of the tree of life, and eat, and live forever. Therefore the Lord God sent him forth from the garden of Eden, to till the ground from whence he was taken. So he drove out the man; and he placed at the east of the garden of Eden Cherubims, and a flaming sword which turned every way, to keep the way of the tree of life.

From the time God sealed Eden, preventing man's reentry, it was only the next generation from Adam that the fruits of his sin began to show their results in the lives of his sons, Cain and Abel. After Cain slew Abel, and after the birth of Seth, the generations increased and the population grew rapidly. With this population growth, Satan increased his efforts to claim possession of man, the earth, and its creation. He had created physical and spiritual wickedness with his temptations, deceit, lies, and corrupt practices.

This did not go unnoticed by God, and neither would it go unpunished. Genesis 6:7 says, "And the Lord said, I will destroy man whom I have created from the face of the earth, both man, and beast, and the creeping thing, and the fowls of the air; for it repenteth me that I have made them." These are some of the saddest words in the Bible. They represent God's disappointment, the depth of man's sin and degradation, and the degree of Satan's accomplishments.

Had it not been for one righteous man, Noah, the scene presented in Genesis 1:2 would have been repeated. "And the earth was without form and void; and darkness was upon the face of the deep."

Genesis 6:8 says, "But Noah found grace in the eyes of the Lord." Why? Verse 9: "Noah was a just man and perfect in his generations, and Noah walked with God."

The word *but* places an eternal restraint on the final execution of verse 7. This tiny three-letter word honors the moral, mental, physical, and spiritual nature of this one man and his mentor.

What a contrast this one man was from all other men on earth, as God had described them in verse 5. What God had seen in the ways of all other men was wickedness, which was corrupting their minds and hearts and creating reality out of their evil imaginations and thoughts. Verse 12 describes this reality in action. "And God looked upon the earth, and, behold, it was corrupt; for all flesh had corrupted his way upon the earth."

God walked *with* Noah, but He only walked *among* other men. What a great contrast this presents. He knew the thoughts of their minds, the imaginations of their hearts, and how this became reality in their actions. Those three things represent their flesh (actions), their moral nature (thoughts of their minds), and their spiritual nature (imaginations or intents of their hearts). These three conditions represent the total depravity of the human race only a few generations from the time of man's creation. How subtly, how powerfully, how diligently, and how deceitfully Satan had worked among those whom God initially created without sin.

Noah was not the only man God had walked with. It is evident that God had walked with Adam before he sinned. After they had sinned, Adam and

Eve were alarmed when they heard God walking and talking with them, because their conscience had been awakened by their disobedient action and their guilt and shame created the fear of God (Genesis 3:9–11). This was the first time God's walking and talking with them threatened a judgmental action, creating their fear.

Genesis 5:22–24 records another man who walked with God.

> And Enoch walked with God after he begat Methuselah three hundred years, and begat sons and daughters. And all the days of Enoch were three hundred sixty and five years. And Enoch walked with God: and he was not; for God took him.

Look briefly at this pattern. Adam, as the first man, was the progenitor of all generations of fallen man who would follow him. Romans 5:12 says, "Wherefore, by one man sin entered into the world, and death by sin." In the midst of the sin, wickedness, and corruption of all men around him, Enoch "walked with God, and he was not, for God took him." Enoch here is representative of the bride of Christ, who is in the world but not of the world (John 17:14). Noah walked with God, and because of him, God spared the complete destruction of the earth, making it a destructive cleansing with the remnant of man, beast, creeping things, and fowls being preserved through all of it, to inherit, inhabit, and repopulate the cleansed earth. This is representative of those whom God will spare in a place of safety while the final destructive cleansing actions of God are being poured out upon the earth just before, during, and after the tribulation and Armageddon.

Genesis 11–13 reflect the spirit, nature, and works of Satan, and the kind of kingdom he would build with and among men on earth.

> The earth also was corrupt before God, and the earth was filled with violence. And God looked upon the earth, and, behold, it was corrupt; for all flesh had corrupted his way upon the earth. And God said unto Noah, The end of all flesh is come before me; for the earth is filled with violence through them; and, behold, I will destroy them with the earth.

How utterly different the world had become from the kingdom God had created. Genesis 1:31: "And God saw everything that he had made, and, behold, it was very good." That presents God's work and His assessment about what He had created, but oh, how soon Satan had changed this created work. Satan's power to deceive had not diminished from when he was in heaven. If he could create such havoc in heaven, causing himself and a third part of the angels to be cast out, bound in chains of eternal darkness, ultimately to be eternally punished in the lake of fire, it is no wonder he so soon began his work in the same wicked and corrupt manner with man.

Satan has never changed his purpose, his thoughts, his ways, or his works. His purpose has been to establish his own kingdom in opposition to God's kingdom, whether in heaven or on earth. His thoughts have been to accomplish this through the angels in heaven and man on the earth. His ways are about how this will be done, and those ways are through cunningness, deceitfulness, temptation, lies, and confusion, as an angel of light or as a roaring lion. His works are the results of his purpose, thoughts, and ways. His works are evil, corrupt, and wicked. Evil represents his basic nature. Corruption represents the change that his applied evil makes on things touched or taken over by it. Wickedness represents the results of this evil and corruption.

This trinity was evident in the original conflict between Lucifer (Satan) and God in heaven, as Satan's evil nature exercised itself through its use among the angelic inhabitants, getting them to join him in his actions against God. Satan used this same trinity to bring about the fall of man in Eden, which we have just shown. It is the same thing he used on the first generations of man after God had driven them from Eden. It was these same three types of temptations he offered Jesus Christ in the wilderness temptation (Matthew 4:1–11). It is these same three things he is using on men today that will ultimately bring about God's judgment of the great tribulation spoken of in Daniel 12 and in the book of

Revelation. It will be these same three things Satan will use when he is "loosed for a little season" at the end of the millennial reign of Jesus Christ.

> And when the thousand years are expired, Satan shall be loosed out of his prison. And shall go out to deceive the nations which are in the four quarters of the earth, Gog and Magog, to gather them together to battle: the number of whom is as the sand of the sea. And they went up on the breadth of the earth, and compassed the camp of the saints about, and the beloved city: and fire came down from God out of heaven, and devoured them.
>
> Revelation 20:7–9

In the midst of all this spiritual, moral, and physical carnage that Satan has brought upon man, God yet maintains some who worship Him, walk with Him, talk with Him, and will receive the ultimate reward of eternal life with Him in the new heaven, or as the inheritors and inhabiters of the new earth. Revelation 21:1 says, "And I saw a new heaven and a new earth: for the first heaven and the first earth were passed away; and there was no more sea."

It seems in every thousand-year period, God has a remnant, and they can be identified as examples of individuals with the righteousness of God dwelling in them. Many could be named, but here are a few as examples. In the first thousand-year period, we see Enoch and Noah as men God clearly identifies as this kind of an example. In the second thousand-year period, we see Abraham and Moses as men God clearly identifies as this kind of an example. In the third thousand-year period, we see Elijah, David, and Job as men God clearly identifies as this kind of an example. In the fourth thousand-year period, we see Isaiah, Daniel, and Ezekiel as men God clearly identifies as this kind of an example. In the fifth thousand-year period, we see the disciples, Paul and Stephen, as men clearly identified as this kind of an example. In the sixth thousand-year period, we see the martyrs, Martin Luther and Charles Wesley, as men clearly identified as this kind of an example. We do not know when it will begin, but during the tribulation, there will be others who could fit this example.

In spite of everything, God will ultimately restore a sinless earth to a sinless generation. They will inhabit it and fulfill God's command to Adam and Eve, that was repeated to Noah and his sons. "Be fruitful, and multiply and replenish the earth" (Genesis 1:28 and Genesis 8:17).

God's Destructive Action Against Sin

Because the wickedness of man had corrupted his mind, heart, and ways (Genesis 6:5 and 12) and the earth was filled with violence (verse 13), God's patience and tolerance would no longer prevent His justice and judgment from being executed against "all flesh that was upon the earth." God spoke to Noah and said, "The end of all flesh is come before me," and He sadly announced, "I will destroy them with the earth."

He extended mercy to Noah and his family because of the righteousness of Noah. This mercy brought with it instructions on how to build an ark that represented the only salvation from this universal destructive action. In obedience, Noah built this ark as the means of preservation for him, his family, and "of every living thing of all flesh, two of every sort shalt thou bring into the Ark, to keep them alive with thee, they shall be male and female.

Of fowls after their kind, and of cattle after their kind, of every creeping thing of the earth after his kind, two of every sort shall come unto thee, to keep them alive" (Genesis 6:19–20). Noah didn't have to go searching for them or gather them up, for God said, "Two of every sort shall come unto thee."

Noah was one hundred twenty years in building the ark. This was a period of grace, with Noah and his work being a witness to all people of God's impending wrath and destruction that was coming upon all the earth. That period of grace did not open their eyes to their wickedness, to God's anger and grief because of that wickedness, or to their own impending destruction. The sounds of their wicked ways and the laughter from their indulgences in the pleasures of sin drowned out God's warning. "My spirit shall not always strive with man" (Genesis 6:3). Only Noah and his family served God, while all other mortals on the earth served the desires of the flesh. Such a corrupt, ungodly, and violent environment is hard for us to imagine, even though more and more we are seeing the days of Noah being repeated.

The wise men and the men of science must have opposed Noah's prophecy of an impending flood, because there was nothing in all of their history or in the known laws of nature and scientific knowledge that indicated such a universal deluge was possible. It was, to them, only the fanciful imagination and distortions of this mentally deranged old man and nothing for them to fear.

With the ark completed, God instructed Noah and his family to enter the ark. It also appears all of the pairs of creatures God would preserve with Noah were compelled by the Lord to enter the ark.

Genesis 7:1–5:

> And the Lord said unto Noah, Come thou and all thy house into the ark; for thee have I seen righteous before me in this generation. Of every clean beast thou shalt take to thee by sevens, the male and his female: and of beasts that are not clean by two, the male and his female. Of fowls also of the air by sevens, the male and the female; to keep seed alive upon the face of all the earth. For yet seven days, and I will cause it to rain upon the earth forty days and forty nights; and every living substance that I have made will I destroy from off the face of the earth And Noah did according unto all that the Lord commanded him.

The clean beasts and fowls of the air were to be taken into the Ark by seven pairs each, yet the unclean were to be taken only by two, a male and his female. Why this difference? It must have been because God wanted Noah to offer blood sacrifices to Him after the flood was over. Genesis 8:20 says, "And Noah builded an altar unto the Lord; and took of every clean beast, and of every clean fowl, and offered burnt offerings on the altar." As these offerings were burning upon the altar, their smoke ascended to heaven. "And the Lord smelled a sweet savour; and the Lord said in his heart, I will not again curse the ground any more for man's sake; for the imagination of man's heart is evil from his youth; neither will I again smite any more every thing living, as I have done." Just as God had honored Noah's obedience before the flood, He was honoring his worship after the flood and all of the earth would be blessed by it.

What mixed feelings Noah must have been experiencing. He had obeyed God's command in spite of the mockery and ridicule he had taken. After one hundred and twenty years of faithful obedience, he and his family were now entering the ark, knowing all of those to whom he had witnessed were facing certain death. His sense of satisfaction for obedience must have been tempered by his sense of failure to bring only his wife, his sons, and their wives into the ark with them.

As the creatures entered the ark by pairs and sevens, Noah must have marveled at their obedience to the Lord's commands and grieved that man was not as obedient as these creatures.

God gave him seven days for all of this to take place. This was extending God's warning and invitation by seven days to those who had known about Noah and what he had been doing for the past one hundred and twenty years. God was offering them mercy, grace, and repentance one last time.

At the end of the seven days, the great door of the ark seemed to close by itself. Genesis 7:16: "And the Lord shut him in." Only the sound of its closing broke the silence that surrounded the ark. All of this had taken place without anyone but Noah and his family observing it. The crowds had become so familiar with reports of Noah's activities and warnings they had long since lost interest in it and didn't care to hear anything about what was happening to this old man and his ark. They continued in their pleasures, in their eating and drinking, in their marrying and giving in marriage. They continued in their violence and corrupt ways, "until the day that Noah entered into the Ark. And knew not until the flood came and carried them all away, so shall also the coming of the son of man be" (Matthew 24:38–39). This prophetic comparison should be a warning to us.

Immediately following God's closing of the ark's door, the skies darkened and thunder began to roll. They had never seen or heard this before. It must have stopped them instantly. Their loud, boisterous laughter changed to whispers. As the windows of heaven opened and the rains began to fall, their whispers changed to panic and pleas for help. As God broke up the fountains of the deep, and the waters from under the ground and from the seas began to flood the land in giant waves, the people were thrown into the waves while also being pounded by the torrents of wind driven rains from above. As the seas convulsed and the waters of the deep began to cover the high places, it was also safely bearing the ark and its inhabitants upon the waters.

Genesis 7:17–20:

> And the flood was forty days upon the earth; and the waters increased, and bare up the ark, and it was lift up above the earth. And the waters prevailed, and were increased greatly upon the earth; and the ark went upon the face of the waters. And the waters prevailed exceedingly upon the earth; and all the high hills that were under the whole heaven, were covered. Fifteen cubits upward did the waters prevail; and the mountains were covered.

Notice the progressive stages of the water upon the earth. First, "the waters increased." Then they were increased greatly. Next, they prevailed exceedingly. And finally, "All the high hills that were under the whole heaven were covered." In this brief period, God was giving them time to repent. Did any repent, or did they curse God and defy Him? Only eternity will tell. The closing of the ark's door ended their opportunity for safety from the waters, but God was also ending His period of mercy and grace and they were left to their fate, because, "My spirit shall not always strive with man" (Genesis 6:3). How sad this will be when the door of salvation is closed and God withdraws His mercy and grace at the end of the tribulation. The time of the Gentiles will be fulfilled and judgment without mercy will prevail.

God's judgment against sinful men was being completed and every creature was suffering the same fate as man. Genesis 7:21–23 says,

And all flesh died that moved upon the earth, both of fowl, and of cattle, and of beast, and of every creeping thing that creepeth upon the earth, and every man. All in whose nostrils was the breath of life, of all that was in the dry land died. And every living substance was destroyed which was upon the face of the ground, both man, and cattle, and the creeping things, and the fowl of the heaven; and they were destroyed from the earth; and Noah only remained alive, and they that were with him in the ark.

Notice the completeness of this destruction: "All in whose nostrils was the breath of life," and the vegetation, "every living substance that was upon the face of the ground."

When the forty days of rain stopped, the flood-waters were upon the earth for "an hundred and fifty days" (verse 24). As these days came to a close, except for the ark, the earth looked much like it did when God began its recreation in Genesis 1:2: "And the earth was without form and void, and darkness was upon the face of the deep." The difference was, in Genesis 1:9–13, on the third day of creation, at God's command, the waters were gathered together unto one place and then the dry land and vegetation appeared. In Genesis 8:5, after the rains stopped, by the natural process, on the first day of the tenth month, "were the tops of the mountains seen." From that time, it was twenty-one more days before Noah knew the waters had receded enough for the former trees to be seen (Genesis 8:11–12). In verses 13–14, the dry land was presented to Noah, and from there the ark was emptied and the resettlement of the earth began.

Noah and his family were to be fruitful and multiply and replenish the earth. The same was to happen with all of the other creatures. The first things Noah did was to build "an altar unto the Lord; and took of every clean beast, and of every clean fowl, and offered burnt offerings on the altar" (verse 20). In verses 21–22, God accepted these sacrifices and made a vow to Himself that this would never happen again. He would then make this vow into a covenant with Noah, to his sons and to all future generations (Chapter 9:8–17). The token that would confirm this vow and covenant was the rainbow that God would set in the clouds.

From this time on, the reestablishment of God's purpose for all created things on the earth began to be fulfilled, even though there were troubles along the way. "And Noah lived after the flood three hundred and fifty years. And all the days of Noah were nine hundred and fifty years, and he died."

The future generations of man on the earth now would come from the three sons of Noah and their wives.

God's Judgment against Man at Babel

As we mentioned previously, after the flood, the whole earth was populated by descendants of the sons of Noah. Genesis 9:19: "These are the three sons of Noah: and of them was the whole earth overspread." And thus, "the whole earth was of one language, and of one speech" (Genesis 11:1).

They multiplied rapidly and journeyed to other parts of the world to establish cities, to become nations, and ultimately to become a civilization. As they began to build these cities, nations, and civilization, their humanity began to exert itself and influence their spirit, their mind, their self-image, and their relationship with God.

In Genesis 10, we found the generations of the sons of Noah. It is interesting to note that only Nimrod is given space to be described (verses 8–10). Verse 8: "And Cush begat Nimrod: he began to be a mighty one in the earth." This presents him as a leader of men, one with influence, power, and authority. This brief statement about him provides insight into what would soon become a source of anger and disappointment to God. Verse 9 says, "He was a mighty hunter before the Lord: wherefore it is said, Even as Nimrod the mighty hunter before the Lord." The people were impressed and influenced by his mighty hunting prowess and considered it with respect from God. However, it would soon be revealed that Nimrod personally considered it his own talent and would use it as a part of his defiance against God and His rule over them.

Chapter 11 takes us to the land of Shinar, where Nimrod and his people dwelt. Verses 3–4 say,

> And they said one to another, Go to, let us make brick, and burn them thoroughly. And they had brick for stone, and slime had they for mortar. And they said, Go to, let us build us a city and a tower, whose top may reach unto heaven; and let us make us a name, lest we be scattered abroad upon the face of the whole earth.

How quickly Satan can influence man to turn inward and away from God. Notice the personal pronouns: they, we and us. God was left entirely out. They consulted with one another, not with God. They would make their own materials, needing nothing from God. The city and tower they would build would become their personal possession. The tower would reach unto heaven, a defiance in the face of

God. They would make themselves a name, separating themselves by name from the lineage of Noah. This would sever ties to the righteous man whom God had spared from the flood's destruction, and place Nimrod as the one whose name would become the one they and their children would identify with. They also believed this would preserve them and they would not be scattered across the earth.

How do we know Nimrod was their leader, and was leading them in a selfish task? Chapter 10, verse 10 says, "And the beginning of his kingdom was Babel." The words *families, tongues, lands,* and *nations* had been used in chapter 10:31. Verse 32 tells how the people were divided. "These are the families of the sons of Noah, after their generations, in their nations, and by these were the nations divided in the earth after the flood."

The people with Nimrod no longer wanted to be known or recognized by the name of Noah's son Ham, their forefather. Why? Satan had found one man whom he could influence with a selfish desire, who was recognized by his people as a mighty man, and who had the ability to provide food for his people. Now he would provide shelter, a city, and a name that would clearly separate them from all other descendants of Noah.

For the first time in the Bible, the word *kingdom* is used. The word *kingdom* separates them from a nation. A nation indicates the power, authority, and

leadership is divided among the people, but a kingdom has a king, one man with the power, authority,
and leadership over all of the people. Only God had
been their King, and the whole world was a part of
His kingdom. On the surface, Nimrod, the mighty
man, the mighty hunter, was becoming what God
alone had been, but behind all of this was the power,
cunning influence, purpose, and person of Satan.
God alone was what Satan wanted to be, and he
could not be that if he did not have a kingdom. If
Nimrod could build his kingdom, separated by name
from all of the relationship to Noah, Satan saw this
as his opportunity to continue seeking to achieve
what he had attempted in heaven, in Eden, and had
continued among the people in Noah's day. Satan
envisioned Nimrod's kingdom, the first kingdom
identified on earth, as becoming his kingdom, nul-
lifying the Lord's Prayer. "Thy kingdom come … on
earth as it is in heaven."

In the tenth chapter, the sons of Noah and their
generations are recorded. There is one common statement that links them together, even though they were
living separately and had been scattered across the
earth. That statement is, "these are the generations
of the sons of Noah." This one thing would become a
clear line of demarcation for Nimrod and those who
were with him. No link or credit was made to either
Noah or God. How much more open could they have

been for Satan to use their selfish intents and interests to satisfy and fulfill his own?

Their city would be called Babel, which would later become Babylon. Babylon would become known in scripture from Genesis to Revelation as a seat of wickedness, debauchery, idolatrous worship, and finally the seat of the antichrist and false prophet. Her end will not come until God begins the final cleansing of the earth, as He prepares to establish Jesus Christ in the millennial kingdom.

The subtle working of Satan was not hidden from God; neither was God going to allow Satan to take over the earth and its newly formed kingdom.

Genesis 11:5–9:

> And the Lord came down to see the city and the tower, which the children of men builded. And the Lord said, Behold, the people is one, and they have all one language; and this they begin to do: and now nothing will be restrained from them, which they have imagined to do. Go to, let us go down, and there confound their language, that they may not understand one another's speech. So the Lord scattered them abroad from thence upon the face of all the earth: and they left off to build the city. Therefore is the name of it called Babel; because the Lord did there confound the language of all the earth: and from thence did the Lord scatter them abroad upon the face of all the earth.

Abraham Is Separated from the Gentile Nations

Genesis 11:10 begins the generations of Shem. It would be from this lineage God would select Abram—later named Abraham—separate him from the Gentile nations, and make a covenant with him.

This covenant would be transferred to his son, Isaac. Genesis 17:15–22, verse 21 says, "But my covenant will I establish with Isaac, which Sarah shall bear unto thee at this set time in the next year." God promised it directly to Isaac.

Genesis 26:1–5, verse 3:

> Sojourn in this land, and I will be with thee, and will bless thee; for unto thee, and unto thy seed, I will give all these countries, and I will perform the oath which I sware unto Abraham thy father.

The increase of his generations was promised, verse 4 says, "And I will make thy seed to multiply as the stars of heaven, and will give unto thy seed all these countries; and in thy seed shall all the nations of the earth be blessed." This expands the generational blessing, families, into a national blessing, for all the nations. Isaac would never have to question why this was being done. Verse 5, "Because that Abraham obeyed my voice, and kept my charge, my commandments, my statutes, and my laws."

God then confirmed this covenant to Isaac's son, Jacob.

Genesis 28:13–15:

> And, behold, the Lord stood above it, and said, I am the Lord God of Abraham thy father, the God of Isaac: the land whereon thou liest, to thee will I give it, and to thy seed. And thy seed shall be as the dust of the earth, and thou shalt spread abroad to the west, and to the east, and to the north, and to the south: and in thee and in thy seed shall all of the families of the earth be blessed. And, behold, I am with thee, and will keep thee in all places whither thou goest, and will bring thee again into this land; for I will not leave thee, until I have done that which I have spoken to thee of.

In these verses, God is emphasizing the great expansion of Jacob's generations and promises the blessings to all "families of the earth", again a reference to Jesus Christ.

God then changed Jacob's name to Israel. Genesis 32:28 says, "And he said, Thy name shall be called no more Jacob, but Israel: for as a prince hast thou power with God and with men, and hast prevailed."

God then made this an everlasting covenant to the covenant seed of Abraham after the death of Isaac. Exodus 2:24 says, "And God remembered his covenant with Abraham, with Isaac, and with Jacob." Exodus 6:4 says, "And I have also established my covenant with them, to give them the land of Canaan, the land of their pilgrimage, wherein they were strangers." Leviticus 26:42 says, "Then will I remember my covenant with Jacob, and also my covenant with Isaac, and also my covenant with Abraham will I remember: and I will remember the land."

I call this the *covenant seed* of Abraham because, as was quoted before, God identified these heirs as those who came from Sarah. This establishes Abraham's heirs eternal ownership of specific lands, continues the promise of blessing to them, and finally, that all families of the earth would be blessed through him.

All other descendants of Noah remained under their same family names, nations, and tongues, in spite of Nimrod's attempt to separate from them. God would not fail when He decided to separate out a people from the generations of Noah. He would now separate a people to become His chosen people. They would receive from Him divine protection and blessings, but they must also honor and obey Him or He would send punishments upon them.

The only requirement for this to happen was that Abram must, "Get thee out of thy country, and from thy kindred, and from thy father's house, unto a land that I will shew thee" (Genesis 12:1–3). If he obeyed this one command, in verses 2 and 3 God obligated Himself to Abraham by making him these promises, which He turned into the covenant.

> And I will make of thee a great nation, and I will bless thee, and make thy name great; and thou shalt be a blessing. And I will bless them that bless thee, and curse him that curseth thee; and in thee shall all families of the earth be blessed.

As noted in my book, *Ezekiel's Valley of Dry Bones Lives Again,* these verses provide a *national blessing,* a *personal blessing,* a *universal blessing,* a *generational blessing,* and later would be confirmed as an *eternal blessing.*

The first words of verse 4 initiate the action that would birth the people who have become known as Hebrews, Israelites, and Jews. "So Abram departed, as the Lord had spoken unto him." The world would never be the same. The nations of the earth would never be the same. The kingdoms of this world would never be the same. The people of the nations would never be the same, and the eternal inhabitants of the earth would never be the same. The inheritance of all earth's creation would never be the same.

When Abram obeyed, this promise became a covenant, and this covenant would later be recognized as God's marriage vows to Israel.

Jeremiah 3:14 says, "Turn, O backsliding children, saith the Lord; for I am married unto you." Notice: "for I am married unto you" is in the present tense, not future tense. It was already done. Verse 20 says, "Surely as a wife treacherously departeth from her husband, so have ye dealt treacherously with me, O house of Israel, saith the Lord." This entire chapter deals with Israel's backsliding and God's pleadings with her to return and reestablish their relationship.

The bonds of this marriage could be ignored, violated, frustrated, and adulterated, for which God would send severe punishment or allow others to punish this people, but ultimately and eternally, they would be a separate people, God's chosen people, and inheritors of perpetual generations upon the earth. After all of their long history of rebellion, apostasy, idolatrousness, and being scattered among the nations of the earth, they would be brought together again, established as a nation, and possess the land God had first given them.

Through them, "all families of the earth would be blessed." Notice how individualistic and yet how inclusive this is. "All families of the earth." This is a direct reference to Jesus Christ, who would become the source of salvation to all who would believe in Him, first to the Jew and then to the Gentile. The lineage of Jesus, son of the Virgin Mary, can be traced all the way back to Abraham, fulfilling the promise that "all families of the earth would be blessed" through Abraham's generations. Their history and the fulfillment of the Abrahamic Covenant is in my book, *Ezekiel's Valley of Dry Bones Lives Again.*

They would rise from a "valley of dry bones" to live again as a nation recognized by all nations and kingdoms. The signs of this began in the late 1800s, gaining worldwide recognition in May of 1948, when Israel became a nation in a day. After Armageddon, when Jesus Christ has destroyed all of their enemy nations, they will complete this national restoration when they recognize Jesus Christ as their Messiah.

The Gentile Nations from the Abrahamic Covenant to Christ

The Bible and history provide great details about the people and nations from the time God separated Abram and his generations, through Isaac, from all other nations and people. Within the limited space we have in this writing, we can only briefly trace the highlights of the separation of nations, development of kingdoms, and follow the history of the Gentile world.

After the Abrahamic Covenant, the biblical record traces three specific groups of people. First were the generations of Abraham. Much of the Old Testament, from Genesis 12 and on, was written about them and to them. Because of their frequent backslidings and waywardness, God changed His dealings with them from following their conscience to establishing laws and commandments, by which they were to be governed nationally and their daily personal lives were to be lived. God chose Moses as the person through whom He would give the commandments and laws for this purpose. God then followed by establishing the Levitical priesthood, the judges, and then the prophets as His agents to administer, judge, and declare His will for the people. From this lineage the Messiah, the Savior of the world, would come. These things separated this people and this nation from all other people and nations on earth.

Secondly, the remainder of the world would be made up of two separate and distinct groups, even though throughout much of history they have had great conflicts, separations, and troubles, in most cases and to most people they are all considered the Gentile people and nations.

These are the generations of Abram's seed through Hagar and Ishmael. Sarai had given her Egyptian handmaid to Abram to bear a child, but from this time on, conflict and trouble began.

It began in Hagar first. Genesis 16:4–6 says, "And he went in unto Hagar, and she conceived: and when she saw that she had conceived, her mistress was despised in her eyes." We are not told exactly how Hagar carried out this despite for Sarai. It could have been with arrogance, jealousy, spite, rebellion, and refusal to perform duties that had been her customary service. What ever it was, Sarai was so troubled by it she went to Abram, verse 5: "And Sarai said unto Abram, My wrong be upon thee: I have given my maid into thy bosom; and when she saw that she had conceived, I was despised in her eyes; the Lord judge between me and thee." At this point, Abram rejected becoming involved in this trouble between the two women. Verse 6 says, "But Abram said unto Sarai, Behold, thy maid is in thy hand; do to her as it pleaseth thee. And when Sarai dealt hardly with her, she fled from her face."

With hurt, with some anger, and with great disappointment, Hagar fled into the wilderness. Abram did not come to her defense when Sarai approached him, and Hagar must have felt a lot of hurt. She had not seduced Abram, neither had she engaged in this relationship secretly from Sarai. However, neither she nor Sarai had envisioned how this would change their relationship and her position as a handmaid.

In spite of the wrong that had been done, and regardless of what was happening between all of them now, God was watching everything that was taking place and would intervene. In the loneliness of the desert, in the loneliness of her spirit, and in the loneliness of her person, God's angel visited her. Verses 7–13 says,

And the angel of the Lord found her by a fountain of water in the wilderness, by the fountain in the way to Shur. And he said, Hagar, Sarai's maid, whence camest thou? And whether wilt thou go? And she said, I flee from the face of my mistress Sarai. And the angel of the Lord said unto her, Return to thy mistress, and submit thyself under her hands. And the angel of the Lord said unto her, I will multiply thy seed exceedingly, that it shall not be numbered for multitude. And the angel of the Lord said unto her, Behold, thou art with child, and shalt bear a son, and shalt call his name Ishmael, because the Lord hath heard thy affliction. And he will be a wild man; his hand will be against every man, and every man's hand against him; and he shall dwell in the presence of all his brethren. And she called the name of the Lord that spake unto her, Thou God seest me: for she said, Have I also here looked after him that seeth me?

Can you imagine the shock Hagar must have experienced when this angel of the Lord suddenly appeared to her? However, his kind demeanor, his non-accusatory words, and his question indicating concern about her welfare must have brought some calm to her troubled spirit. Calling her by name, "Hagar, Sarai's maid," let her know she was not a stranger to him, though he may have been to her.

Enquiring about her immediate past and her immediate future expressed personal interest that she would quietly respond to. "Whence camest thou? And whither wilt thou go?" He knew these things, but he wanted to hear them from her, because he was going to give her advice and instructions and did not want them to seem harsh or demanding.

Hagar responded, "And she said, I flee from the face of my mistress Sarai." What a sad picture, what a broken spirit, and what loneliness is reflected in this answer. She had no place to go, no friends to care for her, and no source of support. Everything that had been her life was now gone. The loneliness and barrenness within her seemed to seek comfort from the loneliness and barrenness of the desert surrounding her. Though she may have begun the trouble between them, Sarai's harsh response had not been countered by Abram's response. How unfair Hagar must have felt she was now treated.

The angel then began to instruct, give assurance, and comfort her. "And the angel of the Lord said unto her, Return to thy mistress, and submit thyself under her hands."

Notice, the angel did not ask her to do this, and spoke it in a commanding, not a demanding way. He did not ask her if she would do this, so she could not ask, "Why should I do this?" He gave her no instructions about how to approach Sarai, so she could not ask, "How can I do this?" He gave her no indication about what Sarai would do, so she could not ask, "What will be Sarai's response?" He didn't indicate there would be any change in her duties or work requirements, so she could not ask, "How much worse will she treat me if she thinks I cannot make it alone?" The spirit and words of the angel were conciliatory and assuring, even though he made no promise or comment about how Sarai would react to this return. The spirit of this must have struck a responsive cord with Hagar. She made no negative response.

To provide a positive motivation for this, the angel said, "I will multiply thy seed exceedingly, that it shall not be numbered for multitude." What an assurance that nothing would intervene to destroy this child. The angel gave Hagar further confidence when he said, "Behold, thou art with child, and shalt bear a son, and shalt call his name Ishmael, because the Lord hath heard thy affliction" (Genesis 16:11). By invoking the Lord's name and providing the child's name as being from the Lord, the angel rapidly built Hagar's confidence and any fear she had of returning to Sarai was rapidly being put to rest.

The angel then went beyond the child's birth and began describing its future. Verse 12 says, "And he will be a wild man; his hand will be against every man, and every man's hand against him; and he shall dwell in the presence of all his brethren." This description of him reflects the response of a person whose childhood had been lived in a hostile environment, who had to struggle to survive against those who controlled this environment, but through all of this developed a character that was not weak, did not turn and run from the struggle, but learned to live with the situation, surrounded by those to whom he had relationship, but never friendship.

It was this description, and with this assurance her child would never become lost to the world, that

Hagar found the courage and peace to return to Sarai. Hagar then addressed the Lord. Verse 13 says, "And she called the name of the Lord that spake unto her, Thou God seest me: for she said, Have I also here looked after him that seest me?" She had learned of this God while living in the home of Godly Abram. The angel convinced her she was not alone in this struggle, but that the God of Abram was watching over her, and she needed to turn to Him and accept His watching over her.

As a token of this event, and her turning back as Sarai's maid, the name of the well where the angel found her is given, Beerlahairoi, and its location is given, "between Kadesh and Bered" (verse 14).

She returned and "bare Abram a son: and Abram called his son's name Ishmael," (verse 15). This shows Hagar had communicated her visit with the angel to Abram and that he accepted both her return and the son she bore him when it is said, "and Abram called his son's name Ishmael." Abram did not know what lay ahead, but he was honoring Hagar, the son, and his God by accepting Hagar and his son.

In Genesis 17, God confirms all that He had promised Abram earlier, chapters 12–15. God calls it a covenant and promises to "multiply thee exceedingly." He would become the father of many nations. He changed his name from Abram to Abraham, reflecting this promise. In verse 5, God increases this promise and extends it beyond many nations to "kings shall come out of thee." This represents kingdoms and not just nations. Verse 7 makes this covenant everlasting. "And I will establish my covenant between me and thee and thy seed after thee in their generations for an everlasting covenant, to be a God unto thee, and to thy seed after thee."

God further extends this covenant to include lands. Verse 8 says, "And I will give unto thee, and to thy seed after thee, the land wherein thou art a stranger, all the land of Canaan, for an everlasting possession; and I will be their God." It would not be until after the birth of Isaac, Abraham's son through Sarah, that this covenant would be made exclusively a covenant applicable to Isaac.

In Genesis 21:8–21, for the second time, Hagar and her son are sent away from their home with Abraham and Sarah, into the wilderness. Verse 21 provides a record of the beginning of Ishmael's adult life, his place of dwelling, his becoming a great archer, and his marriage to an Egyptian woman. He is not heard from again until Abraham's death, when he returns, and he and Isaac bury Abraham with Sarah (Genesis 25:9–10).

Ishmael returned to Egypt. His family multiplied and "dwelt from Havilah unto Shur, that is before Egypt, as thou goest toward Assyria." Ishmael died at one hundred thirty seven years of age, "in the presence of all his brethren" (Genesis 25:12–18).

His generations were called Ishmaelites, and later became nations and kingdoms, covering a large portion of land and have become known as Arabs. Their struggle with the Israelites has been an historical struggle. It will become a major focus for the end times and will not end until Armageddon.

All of the remainder of Noah's generations are clearly referred to as the Gentile people and nations. These include the generations of Abraham through Keturah, whom he married after the death of Sarah. They are listed in Genesis 25:1–4. Verse 5 says: "And, Abraham gave all that he had to Isaac." The children of Abraham from Keturah received no inheritance from Abraham.

THE GENTILE HOPE

Genesis 3:15 was promised before Abraham's seed was separated from the other generations of Adam and Noah. From the time God developed Abraham's generations as His chosen people, separating them to Himself, they considered the other generations of man as heathen. John 3:16 bridges the great chasm between Abraham's generations and all other people on earth. "For God so loved the world, that he gave his only begotten Son, that whosoever believeth in him should not perish, but have everlasting life." The words "whosoever believeth in Him" breaks the barrier that existed between Abraham's seed and all other peoples, so any generation, any tribe, any family, or any individual can be saved. Gentiles believing in Jesus Christ as the Son of God and as the Savior of the world will be justified just as much as any of the generations of Abraham through Isaac.

When He came to His own, and His own received Him not, great hope sprang up among the Gentiles. Jesus spent the first fifteen chapters of Matthew ministering to the Jews. In the first verses of chapter sixteen, He withdraws from them, and goes into the country of the Gentiles. Matthew 16:13: "When Jesus came into the coasts of Caesarea Philippi, he asked his disciples, saying, Whom do men say that I the Son of man am?" This name identifies its Gentile nature, coming from the name Caesar. Verse 14 indicates the people did not know who He was. "And they said, Some say that thou art John the Baptist; some Elias and others, Jeremias, or one of the prophets." In verse 15, Jesus then directs His question to His disciples. "But whom say ye that I am?" Verse 16: "And Simon Peter answered and said, 'Thou art the Christ, the Son of the living God.'" Though the general populace and the Jewish leaders did not know who He was, His disciples had come to recognize Him. From verses 17 through 20, He blesses them, empowers them, and charges them. He would now go to all people, which was shown by the many works He did among Gentiles from that time on.

When Saul of Tarsus was struck down on the road to Damascus, God was selecting the messenger to the Gentiles. When Saul, whose name was changed to Paul, received his sight, he was told what his message to the world would be and to whom he was to go. This brought hope to the Gentiles. Acts 13:42 says, "And when the Jews were gone out of the synagogue, the Gentiles besought that these words might be preached to them the next Sabbath."

Verses 44–49 says,

> And the next Sabbath day came almost the whole city together to hear the word of God. But when the Jews saw the multitudes, they were filled with envy, and spake against those things which were spoken by Paul, contradicting and blaspheming. Then Paul and Barnabas waxed bold, and said, It was necessary that the word of God should first have been spoken to you; but seeing ye put it from you, and judge yourselves unworthy of everlasting life, lo, we turn to the Gentiles. For so hath the Lord commanded us, saying, I have set thee to be a light of the Gentiles, that thou shouldest be for salvation unto the ends of the earth. And when the Gentiles heard this, they were glad, and glorified the word of the Lord: and as many as were ordained to eternal life believed. And the word of the Lord was published throughout all the region.

Paul was telling the Gentiles he had been set as a light to the Gentiles "for salvation unto the ends of the earth." This brought joy, praise, worship, believing, and then salvation to the Gentiles. How prophetic this statement is. Since Paul and Barnabas introduced it to the Gentiles, the gospel of Jesus Christ has been spread around the world through the ministries of Gentiles. The Old Testament teachings and religious practices were almost exclusive to the Jews, and because they rejected Jesus Christ, they rejected what He was teaching and, with some exceptions, have continued as a people to follow the Old Testament doctrines, ordinances, and practices.

Since the days of Paul and Barnabas, the Gentiles have become the worldwide ministers of the gospel of Jesus Christ. They have been its recipients, its carriers, its martyrs, and its fruit. There is little doubt the Gentiles have exceeded Christ's own people as the reward of His labors. They have evangelized the world. They have become a major part of His body on earth, the church. They will be a great part of His bride.

Throughout periods of history, there have been dark sides to this picture of the Gentiles, but none so great as its last picture. They have engaged in every conceivable form of wickedness, but their relationship with God is ended because of their spiritual lukewarmness. In Revelation 3:14–22, the message is to the Laodicean church, which is a Gentile church. The message is one of knowledge, appraisal, counsel, warning, and judgment.

Verse 15 says, "I know thy works," is God's knowledge about what that church has been doing. "Thou art neither hot nor cold" is His appraisal of their spiritual condition. "I would thou wert cold or hot" is His counsel. "Because thou art lukewarm" is His warning to change. "I will spew thee out of my mouth" is separation from God as a final judgment.

Verse 17 follows the same pattern. "Because thou sayest" is God's knowledge of the boldness of their words. "I am rich and increased with goods" is His record of their own self and selfish appraisal of themselves. "And have need of nothing" is a reflection of their perceived and deceived spiritual condition. "And knowest not that thou art wretched, and miserable, and poor, and blind and naked" is God's appraisal of them and comes as both a warning and their judgment.

Verses 18–22 extends instruction, help, blessing, the opportunity of fellowship, shared blessings now, and ultimately an eternal inheritance. Verse 18 provides instruction and help. Verse 19 tells them His rebuke and chastening is because of the blessing of His love to them. It also offers the provision of repentance, which is necessary before true fellowship is established. Verse 21 describes the fellowship that begins now and that they will inherit as eternal. "To him that overcometh will I grant to sit with me in my throne, even as I also overcame, and am set down with my Father in his throne."

From this picture of the Gentile church of the last days, we see it no longer presents the true gospel, the true message, or the true example of the body of Jesus Christ to the world. It becomes a carnal, materialistic, self-centered model of a spoiled child. The glory of its beginning becomes that by which it receives its judgment at the end. What it once was it now scorns. What it once practiced it now rejects. What it once preached it now declares as obsolete.

What God once accepted as a part of the body of Jesus Christ, He declares He will now spew out of His mouth. His patience now gives way to punishment. His justice will declare its judgment.

What a sad end to that which had such a glorious beginning. What great eternal loss for that which had such fleeting values. How great is its eternal broken relationship for such valueless friendship with the world.

The words "I will spew thee out of my mouth" leaves the Gentiles open to suffer all of the horrible losses, punishments, and final judgments of the tribulation and Armageddon. They are left alone to face the antichrist and the false prophet, as well as the wrath, fury, and punishment God will send upon the earth when the seven seals are broken, the seven trumpets sound, and the seven vials of God's wrath are poured out.

THE GENTILE VALLEY OF BONES

In the tenth chapter of Genesis, the word *Gentile* is used for the first time in the Bible. Verse 5 says: "By these were the isles of the Gentiles divided in their lands; every one after his tongue, after their families, in their nations." It is from this settling of the generations of the sons of Noah into these isles of the Gentiles that they became known as the Gentile nations. Unlike God's interference with Nimrod's attempt to separate him and his people from identification with Noah, God here establishes these generations of Noah and uses the name of the isles to ultimately establish the Gentile nations, not Gentile kingdoms. Men within these Gentile nations would build kingdoms, but not until God separated Abram from all other nations would anyone become known as anything other than Gentile nations.

From the time God separated Abram and his people from "thy country, and from thy kindred, and from thy father's house," his generations and all of the other generations of Noah, or the Gentiles, have had conflicts and struggles living together on the earth.

When Israel drifted away from God, went into idolatry, disobeyed God and His commandments to them, and later disobeyed His laws as given through Moses, God punished them Himself or allowed the Gentiles nations to punish them. What we must remember, though, is that God has never divorced Himself from them and never will.

One of the greatest prophecies relating to the power, authority, and rule of the Gentile nations is in Daniel 2, the dream King Nebuchadnezzar had, and Daniel's interpretation of it as a "great image, whose brightness was excellent, stood before thee; and the form thereof was terrible." This image represented five different Gentile world kingdoms. These five different Gentile world kingdoms were not the first Gentile world kingdoms. Egypt and Assyria were the first two prior to Babylon.

In Nebuchadnezzar's dream, the image's head was of fine gold. This was the kingdom of Babylon that Nebuchadnezzar ruled. It was a beautiful, wealthy, and powerful kingdom. In 606 B.C., Nebuchadnezzar and his Babylonian army had set themselves against Jerusalem, and after a lengthy siege, captured it. They then slew many of its people and sold many into slavery, but took the wisest and mightiest into captivity. Among these were Daniel, Shadrach, Meshach and Abendego (Daniel 1:6–7).

In Nebuchadnezzar's dream, the breast and arms of silver were representative of the kingdom of the Medes and Persians, under the king, Darius. They would later forcefully take the kingdom of Babylon, and slay its king, Belshazzar (Daniel 5:30).

Belshazzar did not honor God or the things of God. In the midst of a wicked birthday celebration with a thousand of his lords, they were desecrating the sacred vessels of the temple of God that Nebuchadnezzar had hidden away and protected. Suddenly, a hand appeared, writing on the wall in words Belshazzer could not understand. Through the instructions from his wife (Daniel 5:10–13), Daniel was called before the king to interpret this dream (verses 13–16). Daniel recounted his dealings with Nebuchadnezzar (verses 17–21). God then revealed to Daniel, and he to Belshazzar, how the kingdom would be taken from him (Daniel 5:22–29). Verses 30 and 31 provide the brief climax to Belshazzar's rule: "In that night was Belshazzar the king of the Chaldeans slain. And Darius the Median took the kingdom, being about threescore and two years old."

The Medes and Persians would rule until the kingdom represented by the belly and thighs of brass defeated them. That kingdom was the old Grecian Empire under Alexander. As the image developed, each kingdom expanded its controlled territory. Each kingdom also became stronger and more powerful, and left some lasting marks that would be remembered long after those nations were gone.

This Grecian kingdom would rule until the kingdom represented by the legs of iron, which was the old Roman Empire, defeated them, and became the world's ruling empire. This kingdom—or, as it became known, empire—had an eastern and western division, representing the legs of iron. Its rule was much more harsh, much more controlling, and enacted greater military force and legislative power than the nations before it. It was in power before, during, and after the time of Jesus Christ and the apostles. It would develop control over both government and religion. It presents the picture of both the government ruling religion and religion ruling government. Many of the laws of today were patterned after the old Roman laws. Its old religious practices are yet carried out by many across the world today.

There would not be another world kingdom until a kingdom, represented by the feet that were of iron and clay mixed, would come into world power. This would be the final Gentile kingdom on this earth and will be the kingdom of the antichrist.

That kingdom begins its formation from the ten major nations that made up the old Roman Empire and will broaden to become a world kingdom. Its ruler, the antichrist, will receive the seat, power, and authority of this kingdom from Satan. Revelation 13:2 says, "And the beast which I saw was like unto a leopard, and his feet were as the feet of a bear, and his mouth as the mouth of a lion; and the dragon gave him his power, and his seat, and great authority."

This lets us know he will be one who does not come into power on his own past greatness, accomplishments, or world recognition. He will not be a person with great and broad experiences of negotiations, treaties, and reconciliatory powers. His past name, position, and image will not be one that immediately comes to mind when negotiations for a peace settlement between nations becomes the greatest need to preserving man on the earth. With the potential of nuclear, chemical, biological, and electromagnetic dynamic warfare, the position, power, and authority to negotiate these things will come from Satan, the author of evil and confusion.

> Thou sawest till that a stone was cut out without hands, which smote the image upon his feet that were of iron and clay, and brake them to pieces. Then was the iron, the clay, the brass, the silver, and the gold, broken to pieces together, and became like the chaff of the summer threshing floors; and the wind carried them away, that no place was found for them: and the stone that smote the image became a great mountain, and filled the whole earth.
>
> Daniel 2:34–35

Jesus Christ is that "stone that is cut out without hands," referring to His virgin birth.

This dream and interpretation presents a picture of the Gentile kingdoms from Nebuchadnezzar's kingdom of Babylon until Jesus Christ returns on a white horse at the end of the Tribulation and destroys the entire lineage of the Gentile kingdoms. This is what we call Armageddon, and when it is over, no Gentile kingdoms will be left upon the face of the earth. The tribulation is the beginning of these final events and their completion is in Revelation 20:11–16, before the "white throne judgment."

The words of Daniel, "Then was the iron, the clay, the brass, the silver and the gold broken to pieces together" (Daniel 2:35) allow for no remaining Gentile kingdoms on the earth. Everything each of them may have contributed to the other, their history, their political, civil, social, legal, military, financial, and religious systems, powers, and authority are broken to pieces together. This is complete and final destruction. Not one segment of their kingdom, power, or authority is exempt from this complete and eternal destruction. Not one of these kingdoms, nor any part of them, will ever be restored to power again.

Not only are they broken to pieces together, but the stone ground them until they "became like the chaff of the summer threshingfloors." They were not broken in large pieces that could be put back together and form another kingdom. "As chaff" represents their having been emptied of any value to the spiritual harvest of this world, the "raptured Church," and would become a part of the judgmental harvest of this world, the "white throne judgment."

They have no restorative value as seed to build other kingdoms. They have no substance worthy of being retained, so they are carried away, never to rule on this earth again.

This will be the fulfillment of Luke 21:24. "And Jerusalem shall be trodden down of the Gentiles until the times of the Gentiles be fulfilled." The Gentiles lost control of Jerusalem in the 1967 war. Though there may be efforts, through negotiations or warfare, to return all or parts of it to the Gentiles, the times of the Gentiles is near its end. As events unfold in the Middle East today and Israel is being attacked by terrorists, threatened with annihilation by others, and pressured by international forces to give up land and part of Jerusalem, we should be aware that God can end these things quickly with the rapture of the church, then beginning the tribulation and bringing it to an end with the battle of Armageddon.

The clincher that clearly shows the end of the Gentile kingdoms of this world are the words, "And the wind carried them away, that there was no place found for them." They were not preserved or taken to a hiding place where they could be retrieved later, where man could reclaim any part of the broken pieces of what they formerly were or possessed. They will be gone. They will no longer exist. When God says, "There was no place found for them," they cannot later be found and restored. This is a pronouncement of annihilation, not just a defeat or temporary setback.

The only kingdom that will ever be on this earth again is the one that answers the prayer Jesus taught His disciples, "Our Father which art in heaven, hallowed be thy name. Thy kingdom come, thy will be done in earth, as it is in heaven" (Matthew 6:9–10). There will be no Gentile kingdoms within that kingdom, because "the wind carried them away, that there was no place found for them." They are not being reserved or preserved to be restored as a part of God's kingdom when it "comes in earth as it is in heaven." They are gone and there will never be a place found for them.

John's description of the end of the Gentile nations is in Revelation 19:17–21.

> And I saw an angel standing in the sun; and he cried with a loud voice, saying to all the fowls that fly in the midst of heaven, Come and gather yourselves together unto the supper of the great God. That ye may eat the flesh of kings, and the flesh of captains, and the flesh of mighty men, and the flesh of horses, and of them that sit on them, and the flesh of all men, both free and bond, both small and great. And I saw the beast, and the kings of the earth, and their armies, gathered together to make war against him that sat on the horse, and against his army. And the beast was taken, and with him the false prophet that wrought miracles before him, with which he deceived them that had received the mark of the beast, and them that worshipped his image.

These both were cast alive into a lake of fire burning with brimstone. And the remnant were slain with the sword of him that sat upon the horse, which sword proceeded out of his mouth; and all the fowls were filled with their flesh.

The times of the Gentiles are finally fulfilled when this destruction is completed by the rider on the white horse, and they are devoured by every flying bird from around the world. The wind that carried them away is under the wings of these birds as they are "carried away as chaff from the summer threshingfloors."

When Daniel said, "the wind carried them away that no place was found for them", he was describing what John would see after the fowls of the air—whom the angel "standing in the sun" had invited prior to the beginning of this final battle, verse 17—had finished their feast.

Following this battle, not one drop of blood or one piece of flesh will be consumed by creatures who cannot fly. Only those who can traverse rivers, mountains, islands, and oceans can reach this valley of destruction. Birds can travel without paths over land, rivers, islands, and oceans, and they can land anywhere and everywhere bodies are floating in this valley of blood.

It should also be noted that "all the fowls that fly in the midst of heaven" were invited to this feast. This means that even those fowls that never were blood-drinkers and flesh-eaters become carnivorous. What the stone that was,"cut out of the mountain without hands" had ground so fine it was like worthless "chaff of the summer threshingfloors," all fowls that fly in the midst of heaven were feasting on and would carry away, never to be seen again.

Can you picture this multimillion mass of birds, as they settle in on this sea of blood and bodies? Each bird can consume such a small portion of blood and flesh, this valley would look like a quilt of feathered creatures covering a sea of blood.

Following this destruction, Satan is bound and cast into the bottomless pit. He will not be allowed to interfere or interrupt the establishment of Christ's millennial kingdom. Revelation 20:1–3 says,

> And I saw an angel come down from heaven, having the key of the bottomless pit and a great chain in his hand. And he laid hold on the dragon, that old serpent, which is the Devil, and Satan, and bound him a thousand years. And cast him into the bottomless pit, and shut him up, and set a seal upon him, that he should deceive the nations no more, till the thousand years should be fulfilled; and after that he must be loosed a little season.

After Armageddon, after "The remnant were slain with the sword out of the mouth of him that sat upon the horse," and after the fowls of the air have completed their great feast, all that is left of the Gentile nations will be this valley of bones. They will never rise again to rule. All who are represented by this valley of Gentile bones will only rise again when they are resurrected to stand before the white throne judgment, from which they will go into outer darkness, into the lake of fire, where there is weeping and wailing and gnashing of teeth, where the fire isn't quenched and the worm dieth not (Mark 9:43–48). That is eternal death, not life. They will never rise to live or rule again.

With the final destruction of the Gentile kingdoms, the millennial reign of Jesus Christ begins. The Gentiles have no inheritance in that kingdom, for there was no place found for them. When the throne of David provides the seat from which the nations on earth are governed during the millennial reign of Jesus Christ, this represents rule over the nations of the seed of Abraham, and not those of the Gentiles, for they are gone.

The tribulation saints will have been resurrected and will reign with Christ upon the throne of David for a thousand years.

Revelation 20:4–5 says,

> And I saw thrones, and they sat upon them, and judgment was given unto them; and I saw the souls of them that were beheaded for the witness of Jesus, and for the word of God, and which had not worshipped the beast, neither his image, neither had received his mark upon their foreheads, or in their hands; and they lived and reigned with Christ a thousand years.

Final Judgments of God against Man's Sins

From the flood in Noah's day, until the Battle of Armageddon that closes out the tribulation period, there never will have been a time, place, or events that will come so close to totally destroying man from the face of the earth as the final actions of the rider on the white horse. Even this Battle of Armageddon (Revelation 19:11–21), which is a judgmental cleansing, does not bring about the total destructive cleansing that must take place to prepare the earth for fulfillment of the prayer Jesus taught the disciples to pray. Matthew 6:10 says, "Thy kingdom come, Thy will be done in earth, as it is in heaven." That will require a literal physical, political, cultural, and spiritual cleansing.

One thousand years later, the events that follow the millennial reign of Jesus Christ will culminate in the destructive cleansing of sinful man, sinful nature, sinful actions, and Satan, sin's source, from the face of the earth.

Revelation 20:7–9 says,

> And when the thousand years are expired, Satan shall be loosed out of his prison. And shall go out to deceive the nations which are in the four quarters of the earth, Gog and Magog, to gather them together to battle: the number of whom is as the sand of the sea. And they went up on the breadth of the earth, and compassed the camp of the saints about, and the beloved city: and fire came down from God out of heaven, and devoured them.

These are mortals, born during the millennial reign with the inherited sin nature, and who were brought up under the rod of iron rule of Jesus Christ and the resurrected tribulation saints, who shall reign with Him for a thousand years, upon the throne of David in the restored earthly Jerusalem.

For the first time in their lives, they will hear the voice, feel the influence, and face the deceitful spirit, words, and person of Satan. A thousand years confinement in the bottomless pit will not have weakened Satan's purpose or power to deceive.

God will keep His covenant with Noah to never again destroy the creation on earth by a flood. He declared the next time it would be destroyed by fire, and that fire comes after the millennial reign, followed by Satan being bound and cast into the lake of fire (Revelation 20:10). In verse 9, God sends fire from heaven to destroy all of those who became Satan's followers after he is loosed from the bottomless pit and deceives the nations (Revelation 20:7). The white throne judgment follows this (Revelation 20:11–15), and when it is completed there will never be another sin or sinner on the earth. As I just stated, God will cast death and hell into the lake of fire. They are the judgments against sin and when there will be no more sin or sinners, He doesn't need them anymore, so they are eternally banished from the earth.

The final act will be when the curse is removed from the earth (Revelation 22:3). That final act of cleansing will restore the earth to its pre-cursed condition, preparing it for the eternal habitation of the seed of Abraham, through Isaac, building God's "kingdom in earth as it is in heaven," and of His kingdom "there shall be no end." The time of the Gentiles will have long since been fulfilled and the kingdoms of the Gentiles will no longer exist.

> And, behold, I come quickly; and my reward is with me, to give every man according as his work shall be. I am Alpha and Omega, the beginning and the end, the first and the last.
>
> Revelation 22:12–13

> Even so, come, Lord Jesus.
>
> Revelation 22:20

listen|imagine|view|experience

AUDIO BOOK DOWNLOAD INCLUDED WITH THIS BOOK!

In your hands you hold a complete digital entertainment package. In addition to the paper version, you receive a free download of the audio version of this book. Simply use the code listed below when visiting our website. Once downloaded to your computer, you can listen to the book through your computer's speakers, burn it to an audio CD or save the file to your portable music device (such as Apple's popular iPod) and listen on the go!

How to get your free audio book digital download:

1. Visit www.tatepublishing.com and click on the e|LIVE logo on the home page.
2. Enter the following coupon code:
   8d7f-8770-0a2d-43ca-db58-f4a8-e886-1689
3. Download the audio book from your e|LIVE digital locker and begin enjoying your new digital entertainment package today!